INCULTURATION

Working Papers on Living Faith and Cultures

edited by

Arij A. Roest Crollius, S.J.

XVI

CENTRE "CULTURES AND RELIGIONS" - PONTIFICAL GREGORIAN UNIVERSITY

YUNUS EMRE: SPIRITUAL EXPERIENCE AND CULTURE

INTERNATIONAL SEMINAR
Rome, November 6-9, 1991
Gregorian University
and
University of Ankara

ROME 1994

ISBN 88-7652-674-9

Editrice Pontificia Università Gregoriana
Piazza della Pilotta, 35 - 00187 Roma

TABLE OF CONTENTS

Présentation

Arij A. Roest Crollius, S.J.
Directeur du Centre "Cultures et Religions"

C'est avec satisfaction que nous présentons les Actes du Symposium sur Yunus Emre qui s'est ténu à l'Université Grégorienne à l'occasion du 750ᵉᵐᵉ anniversaire de la naissance du fameux poète mystique turc.

La figure de Yunus Emre est toujours exemple et source d'inspiration de la compréhension mutuelle entre personnes de religions et de cultures différentes. Les études que l'on présente ici mettent en lumière l'ambiance culturelle de Yunus Emre et analysent certains aspects de sa pensée. Un contexte plus large des études de ce Symposium est constitué par d'autres approches pour décrire l'expérience religieuse d'Abraham jusqu'à l'époque contemporaine.

Il est évident que l'unité intérieure de cette collection d'articles est à chercher dans la foi monothéiste. Ces études ont donné lieu pendant le Symposium à des conversations et discussions d'un intérêt remarquable.

Le retard de cette publication s'explique par une première intention d'y joindre aussi les résumés des discussions, ce qui s'est montré irréalisable. Nous sommes convaincus, pourtant, que se recueil d'études a sa propre valeur et que même à distance des célébrations de 1990-1991 il est un digne hommage à la mémoire et à l'enseignement de Yunus Emre.

Plusieurs des personnes qui ont pris part au colloque, notamment les deux recteurs, n'occupent plus les fonctions avec lesquelles ils sont mentionnés.

Bienvenue aux délégués turcs

Gilles Pelland, S.J.
Recteur de l'Université Gregorienne

C'est avec joie que l'Université Grégorienne accueille pour la seconde fois le Recteur de l'Université de Ankara, à la tête de cette délégation de professeurs. Le fait que le Recteur Serin ait voulu être présent à cette rencontre témoigne de l'importance qu'il attache à la coopération académique de nos deux Universités. Il me fait plaisir de saluer aussi de façon toute spéciale le Vice Recteur, Madame Sözen, qui a veillé à la préparation de ce Séminaire de la part de l'Université de Ankara.

L'importance de rencontres comme celle-ci dépasse les limites de nos deux Institutions. On peut y voir un signe éloquent de dialogue entre cultures et religions différentes. La publication des Actes du Séminaire tenu à Ankara, l'an dernier, grâce à l'initiative de Monsieur le Recteur Serin, contribuera sans doute à faire connaître ses résultats si encourageants à un plus large public.

Le choix du thème que vous avez retenu est particulièrement heureux: Yunus Emre, expérience spirituelle et culture. Yunus Emre, certes, n'est pas un inconnu en Europe. Déjà à l'époque de la Renaissance, Erasme et Luther ont publié des traductions de certaines oeuvres de ce grand poète anatolien. Il nous reste beaucoup à apprendre cependant sur son oeuvre, ce qui l'a inspiré, sa "mystique", le milieu où il a vécu, l'influence qu'il a exercée jusqu'à nos jours.

La figure de Yunus Emre a été comparée parfois à celle de François d'Assise, qui l'avait précédé d'un siècle. Pour cette raison, le "mysticisme" de S. François trouvera sa place dans votre séminaire. La recherche de points de rencontre vous amènera aussi à examiner la figure si importante d'Abraham dans

1

nos traditions scripturaires. Vous élargirez plus encore le champ de vos discussions en étudiant l'époque de la coexistence de nos deux cultures dans la Péninsule Ibérique. Vous vous intéresserez enfin aux courants modernes du mysticisme.

Nous avons beaucoup à apprendre de part et d'autre sur nos méthodes d'analyse et, plus encore, sur les traditions dont nous sommes les héritiers. Dans ce contexte les discussions des prochains jours vont permettre d'approfondir un certain nombre de questions de fond qui caractérisent notre réflexion et nos recherches communes. Cela représente, me semble-t-il, une initiative qui a déjà donné de beaux résultats, et qui demeure pleine de promesses. Espérons, comme disait un poète français, que les fruits passeront la promesse des fleurs.

Opening Speech

Prof. Dr Necdet Serin
Rector of Ankara University

Being here for this very important event is indeed a great pleasure for our delegation. The academic relations between our universities have created a very strong and friendly link over which valuable ideas, inspirations and perhaps more important than these, understanding and tolerance flow. The more we understand each other the better we see that we need more tolerance and solidarity for the sake of future generations. The most valuable heritage we can leave for them would be a peaceful world. Therefore it is pour responsibility to hear the messages left for us to carry to the future. Ankara University, as one of the oldest and best established universities of Turkey, has always believed in the necessity of knowing the world better by exchanging experience and by contributing cultural and academic fields and therefore, with its traditional approach supports communication between various opinions for the continuity of the global well-being and peace. We consider ourselves lucky for having the opportunity of bringing various aspects of Yunus Emre, the great Anatolian mystic, into light. And as we all know, the ideas of Yunus Emre and many other mystics survived to our time in spite of all pressures exerted from time to time on human thoughts and wisdom. Now, we are happy that the great humanist Yunus Emre has been heard by the whole world with his words expressing the spirit of real humanistic values.

It is indeed very impressing to see how he made highly sophisticated philosophies so easy to comprehend. The main point he emphasized was love. He didn't separate between people just because they had different believes and languages. He said:

The world is my true nation
its people are my nation.

3

The following expressions also indicates how and why he cared for love:

> Whoever has one drop of love
> Possesses God's existence
>
> I am not here on earth for strife
> Love is the mission of my life
>
> We love the created
> For the Creator's sake.

Yunus Emre is indeed universal; he said:

> With the mountains and rocks
> I call you out my God;
> With the birds as day breaks
> I call you out, my God.
>
> With Jesus in the sky,
> Moses on Mount Sinai
> Raising my spectre high,
> I call you out, my God.

On the other hand, Yunus Emre pointed out the spiritual values of human, saying:

> You better seek God right in your own heart
> He is neither in the Holy Land nor in Mecca.
>
> Knowledge should mean a full grasp of knowledge:
> Knowledge means to know yourself, heart and soul.
> If you have failed to understand yourself,
> Then all of your reading has missed its call.

The fruitful cooperation between our universities encouraged another valuable relation. Due to very close and friendly approach of Vatican Ambassador, His Excellency Msgr Sergio Sebastiani, we started another joint attempt taking the advice of Yunus Emre:

> Come let us all be friends for once,
> Let us make life easy on us,
> Let us be lovers and loved ones
> The earth shall be left to no one.

The Jean XXIII Ecumenic Center at the Holy See Embassy in Ankara and Ankara University founded a joint Committee this year, named "Let us be friends". This committee sofar organized two conferences titled «Attitude of Christians towards Islam throughout history» and «Attitude of Islam towards Christianity throughout history». We know this committee will organize further activities of mutual interest to promote knowing and understanding.

4

I would like to extend my thanks on behalf of our delegation for your warm welcome, kind hospitality and all the efforts spent specially by Professor Dr. Roest Crollius for the coordination and realization of this unique and meaningful meeting. Due to its rich content, I am sure the Yunus Emre Symposium will produce fruitful conclusions that can create a reliable and firm basis for further intellectual and academic approaches.

Before I complete my words, I would like to express my gratitude to His Excellency Msgr Sergio Sebastiani, Ambassador of the Holy See in Ankara, and to His Excellency Mr Selçuk Korkud, Ambassador of Turkey to the Holy See for their most valuable support for encouraging us to organize Yunus Emre Symposium jointly.

The Era of Yunus Emre and Turkish Humanism

Prof. Dr Melek Delilbaşı

In this seminar which commemorates Yunus Emre, the Turkish poet who addressed 13th century Anatolia but who is still read and adored in our times because he managed to penetrate into the human soul beyond racist or religious dogmatism, I will present my paper in two parts:

1 - first I will try to draw a panorama of Anatolia at the era of Yunus: this is the time when Asia Minor was occupied by the Turks and when Tasawwuf spread together with the migrating Turkomans;
2 - then I will comment on the tradition of «tolerance» and «understanding» of Turks and I will read some representative samples from the humanistic verses of Yunus.

The Turks started their first attacks on Anatolia in the beginning of the 11th century and the began to occupy and get settled in this new homeland after their victory in Manzikert. Already by the 12th century the western writers started calling Anatolia «Turchia». The Turkish society of Anatolia was divided into three categories; these being the urban, the rural and the nomadic population. The land was *miri* belonged to the state), whereas in the cities the strong Ahis guild organizations helped in maintaining public order.

There is significant information about the flourishing economy and trade of Asia Minor in the 13th century in the works of western and eastern travellers and historians of that time such as Brother Simon of Saint Quentius, Rubruck, Marco Polo, Pegolotti, Al-Omari, Ibn Said and Ibn Battuta.

Cl. Cahen who produced an important historical study called *Pre-Otto-man - Ottoman* described this period as follows:

It is certain that between the ordeals of the early and the later Middle Ages, Asia Minor experienced for about a century (including the beginnings of the Mongol regime) an exceptional economic development such as it had not had before and was not to have again for a long period.

The Seljuk sultanate passed through its best period with respect to political, economical and cultural accomplishments during the first half of the 13th century with Ala'al-Din Kay-Kubadh and took a downward course during the reign of his son Keyhusrev who did not share his father's merits. The popular uprising of Babai in 1240, which was caused because of political and economic difficulties, clearly exhibits the shortcoming of this state.

The reason for this uprising, apart from the religious and cultural factors, was mainly the drastic change that occurred in the appropriation of land; the *ikta* system of the Seljuk land started to be transformed into free hold property. Apart from this, migrating Turks who ran away from the approaching Mongols migrated and entered into Anatolia in perpetual waves diminishing the land which was up to that time appropriated as communal property by the Turkomans.

Following this revolt and after the defeat of Kosedag in 1243, the Anatolian Seljuk state succumbs to the Mongol hegemony. The Mongol occupation on one hand initiated an era of pillage and destruction and on the other hand facilitated the Turkification of the area. The important stages of this development can be summarized as follows:

In the 1230's the Mongols drove out a number of Turkoman tribes from Marangha and Arran and from the Mughan plains in Azerbaijan and they got those areas as the winter quarters of the Mongol tribal forces in Iran. The search for good pasture lands for their herds in marginal areas and the ideal of Gaza (holy war against infidels) toward Christian lands led many of the Turkoman tribes to the mountain ranges in the frontier zones. The Seljuk governors usually send the Turkomans towards the frontier areas where they founded a large Turkoman zone in the northern, southern and western mountain ranges of Anatolia.

The defeat of Seljuk army by Baycu in 1256 caused the flight of Kaykaus to Byzantium (1261). Later in 1277 the Seljuk aristocracy and the Turkomans would make an alliance with the Mamluks of Egypt and start a fight against the «impious» hegemony of the Mongols. The Mamluk Sultan Baybars did not manage to get established in Anatolia and after his departure, the Ilhan king Abaga Han reached Anatolia and caused a massacre and the execution of Seljuk vezir Mu'in-al-Din Pervane who had established peace and order for a short time. These events caused still more Turkoman migrations into Asia Minor.

8

The Arab geographer Ibn Said (d. 1274/1286) estimates the population of these Turkomans who lived in the proximity of the frontiers at two hundred thousand tents in the Tonguzlu (Ladik) region, hundred thousand in Kastamoni (Paflagonia) and at thirty thousand tents in the Kutahya (Cotyaeum) region.

The Sejuk period lasted until the year 1277. Then started the Mongol occupation which initiated a series of political, social and economic crises. The nomadic Turkomans fought without interruption against the Mongols. The Turkomans (who were identified as "wearing rawhide sandals and red felt caps") in 1277, under the leadership of Karamanoğlu Mehmet, captured and occupied Konya for a while after a siege. Mehmet Bey bestowed the throne to Siyavush (Cimri), who was one of the sons of the ex Sultan Izz Al-Din and passed a decree where he declares that starting from that date the language to be used in the palace, in the governmental institutions and in public would be only Turkish.

This decision of Mehmet Bey was a reaction to the unpopular practice of the Persian language in the royal court and in the offices of the state; also exhibiting the fact that the nomadic Turkomans in Anatolia were closely attached to the Turkish culture. Yunus as we know wrote his poems in Turkish; and this shows that in his time there existed a cultured group of people who supported and strengthen the Turkish language as was spoken by the people.

The Mongols recaptured Konya, but by the 14th century the Seljuk state would wither away, giving way to new Turkoman principalities such as the Karamanlılar, Hamidoglulan, Menteseoğulları, Germiyanoğulları and the Ottomans, which were mostly founded in the frontiers and the mountainous areas.

Yunus Emre lived in Anatolia precisely in this chaotic period. The Babai revolt occurred around the years he was born; then followed the battle of Kosedağ and the Mongolian raids over Anatolia, the collapse of Seljuk period, the establishment of new Turkoman principalities, the controversy with Byzantium, the famine and the continuous fighting. In this setting of Asia Minor we see the development of the movement of Tasawwuf.

The Turks who came from the East carried with them a culture which had developed in the Asian steppe together with the Islamic principles and ideals. In Asia Minor, where they encountered old Anatolian cultures they formed a new cultural synthesis. They developed a unique Islamic understanding and a special way of living and interpretation of life, the Tasawwuf, which was mainly based on Ahmet Yesevi who lived in the 12th century. It is well known that during the invasion of the nomadic Turkish tribes into Anatolia a number of influential Islamic organizations and dervishes accompanied the newcomers into these areas.

During the Seljuk period the towns of central Anatolia had adopted a high Persian culture while on the frontiers the dervishes who were called baba, abdal or ahi inculcated heretical forms of Islam derived from Shamanist beliefs and conforming to a tribal social structure. (H. Inancık, Classical Age).

In this way by the 13th century Tasawwuf spread extensively in Anatolia among the city dwellers as well as among the nomadic or semi nomadic populations. The dervishes composed mainly three groups: the Kalandariyya, the Haydariyya and the Yasawiyya.

The dervishes used to settle together with their followers, with their families and sometimes even with their tribes in places they considered appropriate and they founded *tekke*s. Mostly they were granted by the emirs lands, tax exemptions, Christian serfs and often built tekkes. The dervishes also helped in bringing large areas of land under cultivation. Barkan gives an account of the tekke establishing years in his article "Colonizer Turkish Dervishes" saying that the dervishes of these years were competent in starting and cultivating gardens and wine yards and in building tekkes; they did not spend all their time with ceremonies and prayers, but they laboured and did not live at the expense and on the labour of others.

We should infer that the tekke of Tabtuk Emre was a unit of this kind. The mysticism of Yunus Emre should be evaluated and understood within the light of this cultural heritage and the practice of these tekkes. Yunus did not chose escapism when he decided to join mysticism, he did not ran away from this world. On the contrary, he accepted and undertook new responsibilities within a different social and human framework. The tekkes and the understanding which they emitted, played a very practical social role; they constituted a popular reference center for ethical values and everyday guidance. It was also through these tekkes that Muslim and Christian culture came into contact sometimes creating and sharing a common ground of coexistence. Hasluck filled two volumes enumerating countless cases where the followers where the followers of the two religions, many times together with the Jews, shared temples, ceremonies, graves, saints, parables, practices and beliefs.

In Konya the Monastery of Chariton, called Eflatun (Platon) Manastırı by the Turks and which also bore the name of Plato because it was believed that the Plato's mortal remains lay there, had an outstanding reputation and attracted pilgrims from all the neighbouring countries and even city-dwelling Muslim notables visited it. The legend of Plato incidentally became a traditional theme among the different creeds, and traces of this belief have even survived down to recent times.

The tolerance of the Turkish Sultans towards the non-Muslims with respect to religious beliefs and cultural and traditional practices was accepted and expressed by many western scholars (Hasluck, Cahen, Zachariadou, etc.). Christians and Muslims had been living side by side in Anatolia under the rule of Seljuk Sultans of Rum. The lives and the properties of the non-Muslims who had experienced the Turkish rule as practised in accordance to the Fıkıh, were under the protection of Islam. The tolerant approach flourished and widened its application as the Turks became established in Anatolia, where very old civilizations had previously existed. The existing mosaic of cultures was a perfect milieu for exercising a humanitarian understanding and tolerance.

Starting with the Seljuk rule, the Turkish sultans married Christian princesses. This tradition goes back even to Malikshah period. Malikshah and Alexios Komnenos I came to an understanding as they were negotiating a treaty and they decided that a Byzantine princes would marry the Sultan's son. The sudden death of Malikshah however could not render this plan feasible. In a short time though, with the reign of Mas'ud I (1116-1155) the Sultan married a Christian. Thus his son Kilij-Arslan II was born of that Christian mother, the sister of the Count St. Gilles, who kept and practised her original initial religion up to her death. Kilij-Arslan himself was married to the daughter of Mavrozomes who was a member of the Komnenos family. The mother of Izz al-Din Kay-kaus II was also of Christian origin. This kind of cross marriages naturally were taken place among the simple people too.

There have also been Turkish emirs and Sultans who have been staying for considerable time at the Byzantium court as they were captured or sought refuge there. These Turks had the chance to learn the culture and the policies of the Byzantines. We can mention for example Çaka Bey who had established a principality near Izmir and as was mentioned by Anne Komnena, the famous historian, daughter of Alexis Komnenos. He was taken prisoner by a Byzantine commander. He had a special training at the Byzantine court. He could eventually read Homeros in the original and he received the tittle of Protonobilissimus.

Following various internal strives Giyaseddin Kaykhusraw I and his son Ala'al-Din and Izzeddin stayed for a year in the Byzantine palace. When the crusaders captured Constantinople (1204) Kaykhusraw fled to Anatolia and stayed with the mayor Mavrozomes where he married his daughter. When later Mavrozomes took up important posts in the Seljuk state, as we know from the writings of Ibn Bibi, he got married to the daughter of Kaykhusraw.

These marriages might have originated from the polygamic Islamic tradition. However they definitively helped Turks to appropriate a tolerant approach towards the Christians. For example, when the son of Kay-Kubadh, Kaykhusraw II married Queen of Georgia Rasudan's daughter, the princess reached the Seljuk palace with her servants, her private priest and her ikons. Thus she had kept her original religion.

Izz al-Din Kay-Kaus II, who was defeated by the Mongols, had taken refuge in the court of Theodor Laskaris II (1254-1258). In 1257 Kay-Kaus recaptured his throne with the help of the Byzantine emperor but had to flee for help to Mihail Paleologos anew due to internal strives. As we see both the Seljuk sultans and the Byzantine emperors and mayors quite often had to take refuge in the neighbouring courts. The brother of the emperor Johannis II (1118-1142) Isakios had to reach the court of Danishment principality where Gumushtekin rendered the required help, as the coup he planned to capture the throne had failed. Irrespective of the expediency of this assistance the open minded approach of Gumushtekin is well known. As we have learnt from the records of Suryani Mihail, Gumushtekin had ordered a Persian to be expelled from his principality because he had insulted a Christian. The founder of Paleologos dynasty Mihail Paleologos had also lived for a while in Konya with Izz al-Din Kay-Kaus II (1257).

This situation continued during the reign of the Ottomans and quite often the emperors sought help from the Ottomans to solve problems which arose as they strived for supremacy.

One of the reasons that the Christian succumbed to the Turkish rule is the fact that the Byzantium was in a decline. In the 10th century, some emperors such as Romanos Lekapenus and Vasilius II tried to limit the power of the landed aristocracy but they had failed. The aristocracy had extended their land at the expense of the small owners who started to turn to serfs. Various religious and schismatic strives also deteriorated the situation. It was then understandable why there was not a strong opposition from the part of the Christian population to the Turkish rule, which on its part did not exert a pressure on cultural matters and which was applying a lighter tax system than the Byzantine one.

There are also historical records showing that in some cases the change of rule was welcomed by the Christian population. For example, the Suryani historian Mihail recounts that the local people had applauded the first Turks who entered the area. Mateos of Urfa also writes that the Seljuk king Malikshah (1072-1092) had a pius heart open to all the Christians, that it was because this that many cities had voluntarily accepted his rule and that when he visited the area of Syria (1086) the people saw him as a «father». Malikshah with a decree accepted the plea of Armenian Katolikos' Barseg and declared (1090) the priests and monasteries exempt from taxation.

Mihail also writes how he used to visit Kilij-Arslan and how they used to have long discussions on religious matters. The Ottoman sultans continued this tradition. According to P. Wittek who had studied the first years of the Ottoman state, the *gazi* at the frontiers treated the people of the areas which they captured with great tolerance and that it was due to this that "there have not been a cultural collapse in Anatolia neither in the Balkans". According to the same historian, the Turks who attacked and captured the new areas could adapt themselves to the new culture, and that the akritoi (the Byzantine soldiers at the borders) joind them in mass and that many castles and towns had voluntarily surrendered to them.

From the letters of archbishop Palamas, who had been captured as prisoner in 1355 by the Ottomans, we have an insight of the tolerance with which Orhan Gazi and his followers treated the Christians. He writes that the Christians whom he had met enjoyed their freedom and that Orhan had asked and organized some religious discussions between him and the ulema.

The Seljuk sultans had a tendency to have friendly relations with the Pope too. It is known that Kaykhusraw II had addressed the Pope by sending a letter to him. It is probable that Kilij-Arslan also dispatched a letter to the Pope. The representatives of Pope Gregorius IX (1227-1241) and of Innocentius IV (1243-1254) were received cordially in Anatolia.

It is because of this tolerance which prevailed among the Ottomans and due to their policy which originated from this understanding, that people of different race and religions managed to live for centuries together as the subjects of the Empire without being deprived from their cultural heritage.

This «tolerance» unique to the Turks of Anatolia, originated in central Asia, then developed as the Turks came into contact with Islam and later expanded as it met the ancient cultures of Anatolia, creating the understanding which gave birth to poets such as Mevlana and Yunus Emre. These poets are the spokesmen, the representatives in the literary arena of this humane approach, they are the first that put the practice into words. And their words, in turn, gave the meaning and established the principles of the already existing application. These poets are the first *literary* expression of Turkish humanism. The western humanist movement was based on ancient and mostly western cultures; the

Turkish humanist movement carries the imprints of eastern and western mysticism but is based mostly on Islamic mysticism, that is: Tasawwuf tradition.

Mavlana Jalal al-Din Rumi is heavily influenced by the Persian culture and represents the urban section of the society; his verses are a plea to all faiths for unity:

> Come, come again, whoever, whatever you may be, come;
> Heathen, fire-worshipper, sinful of idolatry, come.
> Come, even if you have broken your oaths a hundred times;
> Ours is not the portal of despair or misery, come.

Yunus like Dante and Shakespeare utilized the language of his people. Therefore, he lived through the ages and is still much alive in the language and the sentiment of the Turkish people. The cry of Yunus was against oppression, especially of the rulers, of the landlords and of the wealthy against the unprotected powerless people:

> The lords are wild with wealth and might,
> they ignore the poor people's plight
> Immersed in selfhood which is blight,
> Their hearts are shorn of charity.

His understanding of human brotherhood is simple, straightforward and very clear, because he is sincere in his humane feelings:

> For those who truly love God and his way
> All the people of the world are brothers.

Yunus Emre's mysticism is very much connected with his concept that all men are the creation of Love of God. All men are therefore equally worthy of peace and love on this earth. The coexistence of all religious groups in Anatolia is very characteristically expressed in the verses of Yunus. It is the poet in this case who follows the social reality, but still with a superb clarity and philosophical courage:

> The man who doesn't see the nations of the world as one
> Is a rebel even if the pious claim he's holy.

Yunus Emre's humanism originates mainly from his love for God but like Petrark and the early humanists, he perceives and accepts human beings as the main and probably sole valuable being on earth. He saw Man as a small part, the smallest unit of the Whole, probably of the whole creation, but still carrying in himself all the miraculous characteristics and essence of all creation. Man, irrespective of wealth and social position is so close to the whole creation, is

14

so able and potent to exercise love that he acquires a godly respect, love and importance in Yunus poetry.

Man's supreme value is his «heart», which is able to feel, express and emit love in infinite dimensions. According to Yunus the world itself is full of this wealth. This love is the means to reach the highest level of maturity, to protect man from hate and other vices, to control his pride and thus to reach perfection which is nothing else but the supreme happiness of feeling the cosmic harmony.

> You have a self-image in your own eyes,
> Be sure to see others in the same guise
> Each of the four holy books clarifies
> This truth as it applies to man's affairs.

He is very clear; and so modern and so tolerant towards foreign beliefs:

> We regard no one's religion as contrary to ours
> True love is born when all faiths become one.

Yunus is definitely one of the greatest Turkish poets ever to live. But with his humanistic understanding and approach, he behaved also as the spokesman of all the people of his time who lived in Anatolia – "no one's religion is contrary to ours" –. But he is some times also ahead of us in time. We still have much to learn from him, we still have to put in practice his vision of all uniting love. We still have to understand why Yunus is still adored in his home country, in Anatolia; that is we have to see that humanity still expects the day when all-embracing love will reign, uniting all creatures in a brotherly and peaceful world.

> I am not here on earth for strife
> Love is the mission of my life.

Let me finish with an invitation from Yunus; he calls us to join him in all embracing love:

> Come, let us all be friends for once,
> Let us make life easy
> Let us be lovers and loved ones
> The earth be left no more.

15

BIBLIOGRAPHY
used to prepare this article

ALPAY G., *Yunus Emere' nin Hümanizmasının Temelleri*, Uluslararasi Yunus Emre Semineri, Akbank Yayınları, Istanbul, 1971.

BARKAN Ö.L., *Osmanlı Imparatorluğunda Bir Iskan ve Kolonizasyon Metodu Olarak Vakıflar ve Temlikler I, Istila Devrinin Kolonizatör Turk Dervişleri*, Vakıflar Dergisi, II (1942) 279-386.

BAŞGÖZ I., *Yunus Emre*, Istanbul. 1990.

CAHEN Cl., *Pre-Ottoman Turkey*, London, 1968.

ÇUBUKÇU I.A., *Türk Düşünce Tarihinde Felsefe Hareketleri*, Ankara, 1986.

EYÜBOĞLU S., *Yunus Emre*, Istanbul, 1991.

GÖLPINARLI, A., *Yunus Emre ve Tasavvuf*, Istanbul, 1961.

—————, *Risalet al Nushiyye ve Divan*, Istanbul, 1965.

—————, *Yunus Emre, Hayati ve Bütün Şiirleri*, Istanbul, 1971.

HALMAN T., *The Humanist Poetry of Yunus Emre*, Istanbul, 1972.

—————, *Yunus Emre, Selected Poems*, Kültür Bakanlığı, Ankara, 1990. (The extracts of the poems of Yunus Emre used in this article are from the translation of T. Halman.)

HASLUCK F.W., *Christianity and Islam, II*, London, 1928.

INALCIK H., *Fatih Devri Üzerinde Tetkikler ve Vesikalar*, Ankara 1954.

—————, *The Ottoman Empire, The Classical Age, 1300-1600*, London, 1973.

KÖPRÜLÜ F., *Osmanlı Devletinin Kurulşu*, Ankara, 1988 (3. Baskı).

—————, *Türk Edebiyatında Ilk Mutasavvıflar*, Ankara, 1966 (3. Baskı).

MATEOS Urfalı, *Urfalı Mateos Vekayinamesi ve Papaz Grigor' un Zeyli*, Ceviren H. Andereasyan, Ankara, 1962.

MILLAS H., Ο Γιουνούς Εμρέ, (*The poems and the Era of Y. Emre*, in Modern Greek - to be published.)

OCAK Y., *Babailer Isyanı*, Istanbul, 1980.

ÖZTELLI Y., *Belgelerle Yunus Emre*, Ankara, 1977.

SÜMER F., *Yunus Emre Çağında Türkiya' nin Siyasal, Sosyal ve Kültürel Tarihine Genel Bir Bakış*, Ulusrarası Yunus Emre Semineri, Akbank Yayınlari, Istanbul, 1971.

TURAN O., *Les Souveraines Seldjoukides et Leurs Sujets non Musulmans*, Studia Islamica, I (1953) 65-100.

TURAN S., *Türk Kültürü Tarihi*, Ankara, 1970.

——————, *Türkiye - Italya Ilişkileri I. Selçuklular' dan Bizans' ın Sona Erişine*, Istanbul, 1990.

VRYONIS Sp., *The Decline of Medieval Hellenism in Asia Minor and the Process of Islamization from the Eleventh through the Fifteenth Century*, Berkeley, 1986 (2nd Ed.).

WITTEK P., *The Rise of the Ottoman Empire*, 1938.

Abraham as a Model of Spiritual Experience in Monotheistic Traditions

Prof. Dr Bruna Costacurta

In the biblical tradition, Abraham is presented as a model of faith for all believers. His spiritual experience is delineated as an experience of the relation with the transcendent and the invisible, marked by a radical exigence of obedience in faith.

The Epistle to the Hebrews, an important text of the New Testament that rereads the Old Testament in light of the Christ event, clearly shows this relation between faith and the invisible. At the beginning of its rereading of the story of the forefathers it has this to say:

> Faith is the assurance of things hoped for, the conviction of things not seen (Heb 11,1).

When it comes to Abraham, the Letter refers first of all to his call:

> By faith Abraham obeyed when he was called by God to go out to a place which he was to receive as an inheritance; and he went out, not knowing where he was to go (v. 8).

The emphasis is on obedience to the word of God which requires Abraham to set out and is linked to the gift of the land.

The discourse about the Patriarch continues and concludes with a reference to the sacrifice of his son:

> By faith Abraham, when he was tested, offered up Isaac, and he who had received the promises was ready to offer up his only son, of whom it was said: 'Through Isaac shall your descendents be named'. He considered that God was able to raise men even from the dead; hence he

did receive him back, and this was a symbol (more exactly a *parable*). (vv. 17-19).[1]

Here we will try to understand this paradigmatic spiritual experience of Abraham. Our point of departure will be these two significant moments in the story, namely, the call (as narrated in Gen 12,1-9), and the request to sacrifice Isaac (Gen 22,1-19).[2]

1. Gen 12,1-9: The Call of Abraham

The text is well-known. God asks Abraham to set out for an unknown land where the Lord will fulfil his impossible promise – to make Abraham a great people, to bless him and to make him a blessing for all. The words of God are especially significant. First of all there is a command:

> The Lord said to Abraham, 'Go from your country and your kindred and your father's house to the land that I will show you' (Gen 12,1).

To this there follows a promise centering in the blessing which is for Abraham and, in him, for all:

> 'I will make of you a great nation, and I will bless you, and make your name great so that you will be a blessing, I will bless those who bless you, and him who curses you I will curse; and by you all the families of the earth shall bless themselves.' So Abraham went as the Lord had told him; and Lot went with him (vv. 2-4a).

This seems to be the promising beginning of a happy story, but it turns out to be an event through which God reveals Himself in contradiction. In the story of Abraham, fertility comes through sterility, blessing through an apparent curse, and life seems confused with death. When God intervenes in the life of man, reality and appearances no longer coincide, and the believer is asked to discern, to reread events with the eyes of faith, eyes capable of seeing the invisible.

---

[1] On the relation between the Letter to the Hebrew and Genesis 22, and the influence of Genesis and the Jewish tradition on the Letter, see J. Swetnam, *Jesus and Isaac*. A Study of the Epistle to the Hebrews in the Light of the Aqedah, AnBib 94, Rome 1981.

[2] Literary criticism usually distinguishes different sources in the texts studied in this paper. Gen 12 is said to be J, with the exception of vv. 4b-5 which are attributed to P (see C. Westermann, *Genesis*. Teilband 2: Genesis 12-36. BK I/2, Neukirchen-Vluyn 1981, 167). Gen 22 is generally considered E with certain additions and later changes (see R. Kilian, *Isaaks Opferung. Zur überlieferungs-geschichte von Gen 22*, Stuttgart 1970). Our approach instead is synchronic and takes the final text as normative.

Let us now look more closely at the components of this paradox as they are found in the story of Abraham.

1.1. Blessing and Curse

In the Bible the concept of blessing is connected with the pristine gift of God. God is the origin of life. He causes life to be and gives it liberally to mankind with His blessing. To be blessed, then, means to be fully alive, to live life fully, positively, totally. It means to experience life as good, whole, divine, in all its forms and dimensions.

Thus the blessing finds its first expression in fertility (of men, of animals, of the land), because fertility is the revelation of a life which is expanding, multiplying, and continuing forever through the chain of generation. Blessing also means longevity, health, a harmonious rapport with one's body. It means wealth, which allows one to be open to the enjoyment of life and its gifts. Further, in a fundamental way, blessing is tied to the land. To be blessed means to have a land where one can live in stability and security, where one can build a house, till the soil for food, a place where one can live with a family within a society which protects and fosters the rights of the individual.

In view of this, the command of God,

Go from your country and your kindred and your father's house,

seems to deny to Abraham everything that a blessing entails. No more land, no longer a stable life in his own country, and no fertility since his wife Sarah is sterile (see Gen 11,30). Abraham is called to be a «foreigner», to settle in a land which he does not know and which can never be his native land. He is called to live as an emigrant without roots, without rights.

This is an important point of interpretation. It is one thing to be a «foreigner» temporarily, as a tourist for example, quite another thing to be a «foreigner» definitively, as Abraham who must settle in an unknown land. The latter finds himself in a situation of radical poverty and nakedness, since he enters into a precarious and uncertain dimension. He can never be like the others who are native to the land and especially he can never enjoy the same rights. In a fundamental sense he will always be one who "arrived after the others". The others, the ones born there, will always be before him. Think, for example, of the episodes of the wells which Isaac digs. He digs the wells but the local inhabitants say each time, "the water is ours" (see Gen 26,15ff.).

Abraham thus receives the promise of land as he becomes a foreigner, the promise of descendants ("I will make you a great nation") when he can have no children, his wife being sterile. And he receives the promise of stability and permanence ("I will make your name great") when he must live as an emigrant. In short, Abraham receives a promise of blessing for himself and for others as he accepts what appears to be a curse.

What is asked of Abraham is that he trust the power of God, however inscrutable His ways may be. By faith, Abraham can enter into what seems a contradiction all the while continuing to entrust himself to God and to «bless» Him (to «speak well» of Him, according to Latin «bene-dicere», English «bene-diction»). Thus the blessing is carried within the curse until it changes the curse radically and transforms the elements of death into a promise of life. Obedience which comes from faith is the decisive factor for this transformation and seems to represent something fundamental in every religious relationship with the divine.

We come now to the second point of our rereading of the story of Abraham's call, the relation between death and life.

1.2. Life and Death

The contradiction through which Abraham is made to pass and in which he can experience God, has marked his existence right from the start.

Studying Abraham's genealogy we find something strange which calls for reflection. The text reads:

> Now these are the descendants of Terah. Terah was the father of Abram, Nahor, and Haran; and Haran was the father of Lot. Haran died in the presence of his father Terah in the land of his birth, in Ur of the Chaldeans (Gen 11,27-28).

The important words are, "Haran died in the presence of his father Terah", that is «while his father was still alive».[3] It is not only the death that is reported, but a note is added that emphasizes that something is strange – a son dying before the father seems to be against nature. It is in the natural order of things that a father dies while his son is alive, not vice versa. Abraham's family is thus marked by a mystery of death which attacks life.

---

[3] The Hebrew is *wayyāmot ḥārān ʿal pᵉnê teraḥ ʾābîw*. The phrase *ʿal pᵉnê* when used with a person in the genitive means «in the sight of, under the eyes of». In this instance it emphasizes the fact that since the father can see the death of his son, he is still alive at that moment.

But the paradox is even more profound. The son of Terah dies but he leaves a son, Lot, who represents a prolongation of the life of the father. The father lives in his son who remembers him, resembles him, and bears his name (to identify the son and to call him, one must say, «Lot, son of Haran»). Haran does not die altogether because his son is alive, and then there will be the son of the son of, and so on forever.

So Haran is dead but remains alive in Lot. On the other hand, Abraham is alive but is as though he were dead for he cannot have children who could complete and prolong his life. Appearance and reality do not coincide.

When Abraham is called by God and begins his journey following Him, he is already a man marked by contradiction. He is a man who had already left his land together with his father Terah (see Gen 11,31); and now he begins another journey, he without children, together with Lot who is without a father.

2. Gen 22,1-19: The Sacrifice of Isaac

After Abraham set out on his journey, as we know, the divine promise is fulfilled: the patriarch reaches the land and has a son, Isaac. Actually, before Isaac, Abraham had another son, Ishmael, by his slave woman, Hagar. In this way he sought, by his own means, the fulfilment of a seemingly impossible promise of fertility. But God insists on His way: the true son is another, a son to be born of Sarah. When finally Isaac is born, the promise of God has won out, and Abraham's faith has its reward. But when the tension is lessened and everything seems resolved, a new trial comes – God asks Abraham to sacrifice Isaac. This is the second text we wish to examine, chapter 22 of Genesis.

The very beginning of the text sketches the meaning of the whole passage:

God *tested* Abraham and said to him: Abraham (v.1).

The path of faith, sooner or later, puts man to the test. This does not mean that God takes pleasure in trying a man and places him in difficulties just to see how he reacts. It means rather that the absolute transcendence of God and His total otherness place before a man criteria and ways that are not the man's own. A relationship with God is in itself a test, something unknown which it is possible to enter into only if faith overcomes darkness and fear.

So now Abraham stands before the incomprehensibility of God who is asking him to sacrifice his son, that son who represents the fulfilment of the promise and of the divine blessing.

God said, 'Take your son, your only son, whom you love, Isaac, and go to the land of Moriah, and offer him there as a burnt offering upon one of the mountains of which I shall tell you' (v.2).

There is an echo here of the command of chapter 12,

Go from your country ... to the land that I will show you.

In both cases it was necessary to leave. In the first case Abraham had to leave without knowing where he was going, keeping himself open only to his trust in the promise of God. In the second case Abraham knows where he is to go: the land of Moriah, which is traditionally identified with the hill of the temple of Jerusalem,[4] right in the heart of the territory promised by God. And he must go there to do that which destroys the promise and nullifies the first departure. Abraham had left his country to become a great nation. Now he leaves again to go to do away with his only son, the only one who could have been the source of that great nation.

The first command of God was vague; this one is painfully precise:

Take your son, your only son, whom you love, Isaac.

The words build up like a crescendo with an almost cruel insistence, until they reach the loved name, Isaac.

The Jewish tradition has interpreted these words of God as a kind of summary of an imaginary dialogue between the Lord and Abraham. Thus Rashi, an eleventh century Jewish commentator reports:

God said: *Your son*. Abraham objected: I have two sons. God said: *Your only son*. Abraham replied: Each one of the two is the only son of his mother. God said: The one *whom you love*. Abraham answered: I love both of them. Then God said: *Isaac*.[5]

The scene is heartbreaking with Abraham's pathetic attempt to pretend not to understand, to put off confronting the terrible reality.

---

[4] See Rashi, *Le Pentateuque*, vol. I: La Genèse, Paris ²1971, 133. The name Moriah appears also in 2 Chron 3,1 where it refers to the hill of the temple. Literary criticism tends to consider it a late insertion in Gen 22. See C. Westermann, *op. cit.*, 437.

[5] Rashi, *op. cit.*, 133. See also *Genesi Rabba* LV,7 and *Pirge de Rabbi Eliezer*, XXXI.

But Abraham is a man of faith and, in silence, obeys. Verse three reads:

> So Abraham rose early in the morning, saddled his ass, and took two
> of his young men with him, and his son Isaac; and he cut the wood for
> the burnt offering, and arose and went to the place of which God had
> told him.

The sequence of the verbs is strange, mentioning the cutting of the wood
only at the end, when everything is ready for the departure. Perhaps, as some
scholars have suggested,[6] this is a literary device which, without saying anything
explicitly, allows the reader to enter into the heart of Abraham and to perceive
there all the suffering of the father. It is as though Abraham began to obey the
Lord beginning with innocuous things, making the usual preparations as though
this were a journey like many others. He puts off to the end the unmistakable
gesture which transforms the journey into a tragedy – cutting the wood for the
sacrifice of his son. Now obedience is consummated.

Three days journey and they arrived at the mountain chosen by God.
Once there, Abraham and Isaac leave the servants behind and, alone, begin the
ascent towards death.

Abraham had said to the servants:

> Stay here with the ass; I and the lad will go yonder and worship and we
> will return again to you (v.5).

"We will return". But he knows, and we the readers know, that Isaac must die.
"We will return". Is this perhaps a way in which Abraham, from paternal affec-
tion, seeks to avoid frightening his son? Or is he speaking prophetically, Knowing even in the darkness of faith that God will intervene? Is it the same when
he says to Isaac, "God himself will provide the lamb"? The reader does not know
the answer but can participate in the action together with the protagonists. The
reader shares the anguish of Abraham who must conceal the truth. He also suffers
for Isaac, and would like to warn him of the danger as he watches him, all
unknowing, climbing towards death.

---

[6] See Y. Mazor, "Genesis 22: The Ideological Rhetoric and the Psychological Composition",
Bib 67 (1986) 83-85; J.L. Ska, "Gn 22,1-19. Essai sur les niveaux de lecture", *Bib* 69 (1988)
330-331.

The suffering becomes even greater as the reader follows the dialogue between the two:

> Isaac said to his father Abraham, 'My father'. And he said, 'Here am I, my son'. He said, 'Behold, the fire and the wood; but where is the lamb for a burnt offering?' Abraham said, '*God himself will provide the lamb for a burnt offering, my son*'. So they went both of them together (vv.7-8).

Isaac's question is pathetic, heartrending, and puts Abraham in a difficult position – surely now he will be obliged to tell his son the truth. Instead, the father goes ahead in silent obedience.

Abraham's words are enigmatic. God, the true protagonist, is finally mentioned, with certitude in His goodness, with abandonment to an incomprehensibly mystery in which trust conquers the darkness of the test: God will provide. But there is a certain ambiguity in Abraham's answer, because in the Hebrew the words "my son" can have two syntactical functions. They can be a vocative, as in the translation given. Or they can be in opposition, in which case the translation would be «God will provide the lamb, that is, my son».[7] It is as though Abraham, in expressing his faith, had left slip something of his awesome secret. Again, a literary peculiarity has given us a glimpse of the internal struggle of the patriarch.

And now after the mention of God and of the mystery of what is to happen, a great silence falls. Isaac makes no answer to his father's words; Abraham says nothing more. The pace of the narrative seems to slow and all is concentrated on the essential gestures. In the foreground is the hand of Abraham, the father who is about to kill his son. Verses 9-10 read:

> When they came to the place which God had told him, Abraham built an altar there, and laid the wood in order, and bound Isaac his son, and laid him on the altar, upon the wood. Then Abraham put forth his hand, and took the knife to slay his son.

Here the text reaches its climax. We all know what follows: the angel of God intervenes to stay the hand of Abraham, a ram is substituted for Isaac, the place will become forever a sign of the provident love of God, and the divine

---

[7] Jewish tradition knows this ambiguity. Bowker, in his comment on Targum Pseudo-Jonathan (Gen 22,8), says: "The absence of punctuation (i.e. clause demarcation) in the Hebrew is of critical importance in this verse. It was taken by the Targum as 'God will provide himself the lamb for a burnt offering: my son'" (J. Bowker, *The Targums and Rabbinic Literature. An Introduction to Jewish Interpretations of Scripture*, Cambridge 1969, 231.)

promise is renewed. The drama is resolved but not the enigma of the meaning of the event. In conclusion, let us pause to reflect on this.

As we have said, the text is a paradigm. God is presented as an all-embracing experience, as an Absolute beyond any possibility of identification. The relationship with Him requires a total obedience in accepting a command which leads to a relation with death and demands the renunciation of one's life. It is not a question only of ethical demands which present certain values to a man and require a certain course of conduct; what is at stake is the relationship with what is Absolute and, as such, requires everything.

In this light, Abraham is presented as a model of faith for everyone since he has been able to accept the mysterious paradox. When He demands the sacrifice of Isaac, God seems to contradict His own word of life. Isaac represented the only realization of the divine promise. To kill him was the equivalent of denying the promise. And it was all the more cruel as Abraham had to give him up after experiencing the joy of fulfilment.

Abraham had prayed to God on behalf of Sodom and Gomorrah. He had seen God reveal Himself as ready to pardon many who were sinful for the sake of a few who were innocent (see Gen 18). Now he must accept a God who asks for the life of one who is innocent. The miracle of Sarah's sterile womb that became fertile because God was faithful to His word is now negated. And it is negated by the same word which now causes everything to return to sterility by its demand for death.

God is revealed as incomprehensible, a God who is absolutely transcendent, a God who can never be identified with anything, not even with His gifts, not even with the implementation of His promises.

In the light of Abraham's experience it becomes clear that God can be encountered only in mystery and in the acceptance of total gratuitousness. Everything which comes from God is a gratuitous gift which must be continuously received, never laid claim to. It must always be accepted in wonder and in praise which show that we know that all is His, and nothing belongs to us.

Within this comprehension, God reveals himself as the Word which gives life within death. The Jewish tradition interpreted the episode of the sacrifice of Isaac as a sacrifice which was actually consummated. The Midrash narrative has it that Isaac knew he had to die and that he accepted this, sharing the faith

27

and obedience of his father.[8] And when Abraham stretched out his hand to strike, Isaac died. The story is told this way in *Pirqe de Rabbi Eliezer*, XXXI:

> When the knife was at his throat, the soul departed and went out of Isaac. But when God made his voice heard from between the two cherubim and said, 'Do not stretch out your hand to the boy', then the soul returned into his body, and Abraham untied him, and he stood up on his feet and Isaac knew the resurrection of the dead ... Then he opened his mouth and said: Blessed are you, Lord, you give life to the dead.[9]

The faith spoken of in the Epistle to the Hebrews is here definitely expressed.[10]

Thus Abraham's experience becomes a reason for hope for all believers. God, the totally Other, the transcendent mystery which cannot be named, is revealed as the ultimate gift of life. He is "The Giver of Life". The resolution of the apparent contradiction, of the mysterious paradox which faith must confront, is found once and for all in the resurrection of the dead.

---

[8] This belief is present in all the Jewish tradition. See, for example, *ad loc*, Genesi Rabba, Midrash Wayyosha, Rashi, Midrash Aggada, Genesi ha-Gadol, etc.

[9] The same interpretation is also found in Midrash Wayyosha: see *Il canto del mare. Omelia pasquale sull'Esodo*, a cura di U. Neri, Roma 1976, 54-56.

[10] See also Rom 4,17-22, especially v.17: "(Abraham is the father of us all) in the presence of the God in whom he believed, who gives life to the dead and calls into existence the things that do not exist".

Cultural Background of Yunus Emre

Prof. Dr Sevim Tekeli

There is no doubt that a certain high-level background has always played an indispensable role in the makings of scientists, philosophers and poets in any period of history.

Alp Arslan won the Battle of Malazgirt in 1071, and Seljuks reached the gates of Istanbul soon after the victory. Seljuks, who reigned over a vast area, founded the Great Empire of Seljuks. To Turks, the motherland meant the land where culture flourished. This could only be realized through a widespread system of education. In addition, they believed that education was one of the tasks of the state. This explains why the earliest institutions of higher education on the world were established during the reign of Seljuks.

In Islam the mosque, from early dates on, was not only a place of worship but also a place for instruction and teaching. This teaching depended on personal initiative. It was the Great Seljuks who organized higher education by creating the *madrasa* system, during the reign of Alp Arslan (1063-1072) under the efforts of his Vizier Nizâmûlmulk, earlier than the medieval European universities.

The program of instruction was rather stable in general outline. A library was invariably attached to each *madrasa*. The *madrasa* was not a center of research activity, and nor was the medieval European university. *Madrasas* were built in several countries during the reign of Great Seljuks. The *madrasas* of

Bagdâd, Basra, Nishapur, Herat, Merv, Belh, Amûl, Musûl, Tabaristan can be mentioned.[1]

Beside the *madrasas*, the most important and elaborate observatory of the eleventh century was founded by Malikshâh (1072-1092). He gathered eminent astronomers as Omar Ibn Ibrahim al-Khayyam, and Abû'l Muzaffar al-Asfizarî. This observatory lasted nearly twenty years. Therefore we can say that this observatory is quite remarkable for its relative longevity.[2]

They prepared a new solar calender bearing the name *tarih-i Jâlâlî*. The beginning of the year was at the vernal equinox of 1075.

As it is known, the algebraist of special prominence among not only the Muslims but the world, in the 12th century, was Omar Khayyam. The first noteworthy attempt at a systematic classification is found in his algebra, *Fi'l Berahinî al-nesail al-Jebr ve'l mukabala*.[3]

After presenting his entire classification Omar Khayyam states that numerical solutions for the cubic equations are impossible, but by means of the intersection of conic sections he can give geometric solution to each, that is to say thirteen forms.[4]

The algebraic solution of these forms had been discovered by Tartaglia, the Venetian mathematician in 16th century. Cardano tried to obtain permission to print it, but Tartaglia refused to print it, but he confined the solution to Cardano, who swore to keep it secret. In 1545 appeared Cardano's book *Artis magnae sive de regulis algebraicis* in which the algebraic solutions of the cubic equations of Tartaglia were included.

Binomial theorems: The development of $(a+b)^n$ for any integral value of n was known by Khayyam; as Smith says in his *History of Mathematics*

> The development of $(a+b)^n$ for any integral value of n, or at least a device for finding the coefficients, was known in the East long before it appeared in Europe.

---

[1] Ayalla Sayılı, Turkish Contributions to ?? and Reform in Higher Education, and Hüseyin Rıfkı and his Work in Geometry. *Annals de l'Université d'Ankara*. Tome XII. 1966 (Ankara 1972), p. 89-98.

[2] A. Sayılı, *The Observatory in Islam and its Place in the General History of the Observatory*. Ankara 1960, p. 160-166.

[3] Vaqar Ahmed Rizvî, *Umar Khayyan as a Geometrician - A Survey*. Islamic Studies. Vol. XXIV, No. 2 (1985) p. 197.

[4] V.A. Rızvî, p. 198.

The case of n = 2 was also known to Euclid; but any evidence of the generalization of *n* fist appeared so far as we know, in the algebra of Omar Khayyam. This writer did not give the law, but he asserted that he could find the fourth, fifth, sixth and higher roots of numbers by a law that he had discovered and which did not depend upon geometric figures.[5]

The question of Euclid's fifth postulate, relating to the parallel lines, has occupied the attention of geometers ever since the elements was written. The first scientific investigation of this part of the foundation of geometry was made by Saccheri (1733), a work which was not looked upon as a precursor of Labechevsky however, until Beltrami (1889) called attention to the fact.

Recent researches show that Omar Khayyam also tried to prove the 5th postulate. In his proof he followed the way of Saccheri.[6]

Further developments were realized during the reign of Malikshah's sons. The evidence for any major development after Malikshah is Al-Khâzinî's observatory in Marw, founded for Sanjar (d.1157).

Abû Mansûr' Abd al-Rahmân al-Khâzinî prepared an astronomical table, called *Al-Zîj al-Mu'tabar al-Sanjarî*. This astronomical table is very elaborate and contains several topics of astronomy as comparison of observed and calculated positions of all planets as well as the sun and the moon at conjunctions and eclipses. Beside the scientific value, this table played an important role in the transmission of scientific knowledge to the west and continuation of intellectual pursuits.

Heiberg in his *Byzantinische Analecten*, gave a short description of codes Vat.Gr. 1058. In this codex there are several astronomical manuscripts among which there is one, named *A big astronomical work* written in 15th century. Neugebauer, in the *Studies in Byzantine Astronomical Terminology*, says that this is the Greek translation of *Sanjarî Zîj*. But it shows rather a composite character, related to *Alai Zîj, Ilkhanî Zîj* beside the *Sanjarî Zîj*.[7]

The Seljuks who came to the door of Istanbul were the carriers of such a great culture. As the time is limited let us go to the 13th century in which Yunus Emre was born.

[5] D.E. Smith, *History of Mathematics*. Vol. 2, New York 1951.

[6] *op. cit.*, p. 336.

[7] O. Neugebauer, "Studies in Byzantine Astronomical Terminology." *Transactions of the American Philosophical Society*, New Series. Vol. 50, Part 2 (1960), p. 4, 31.

First of all I shall dwell on the institutions of education. More than one *madrasa* were built in one city. Ibn Jubair (580-1184) states that in his time there were 30 *madrasas* in Bagdâd,[8] every one of which could compare with the most splendid palace.

A little earlier than Yunus Emre, in Diyarbakır lived Al-Jazarî, a leading engineer. Very little is known about his life story. He was in the service of Nasir al-Dîn, the Artuqid, king of Diyarbakır. He spent twenty five years in the service of this family. He wrote his famous book named *The Book of Knowledge of Ingenious Mechanical Devices* for Nasir al-Dîn. Donald R. Hill translated this book into English, with a foreword by Lynn White. It includes several water clocks, vessels and figures suitable for drinking, pitchers, fountains, perpetual flutes, and machines for raising water. One of his monumental water clocks was accurately reconstructed for the Science Museum, London for the year 1976 World of Islam Festival. Now I am going to give a very brief explanation of this clock.

This water clock consists of a house about 10 feet square by 11 feet high. In this house there is a door, which is closed by a wall of wood or bronze. Above the door, in a lateral straight line, are 12 doors, each of which has two leaves which are closed at the beginning of the day. Below these, and parallel to them are 12 more doors, each with one leaf, which all have the same colour at the beginning of the day. Below the second set of doors, in either side of the wall is a niche like a *mihrab* and in each of these is a bird with outstretched wings, standing on its feet. Between the two niches are 12 roundels made of glass, which are so arranged that they form a semicircle with its convex side upwards. In front of each bird is a vase supported on projecting bracket and in each vase is hung a cymbal, below the wall several figures are situated: two drummers, two trumpeters and a cymbalist. Above the wall is a semi circle with its convexity towards the top. Around its circumference are six of the 12 Zodiacal Signs, below this, is a sphere carrying the sun, and below this, a sphere carrying the moon.

At the end of one hour the two panels of the first of the upper doors open and a figure comes out. Also the first door turns over and changes colour, the two birds lean forward until they approach the two vases, and two balls are dropped from their beaks, each on to a cymbal and the sound is heard from afar. The birds then resume their position. This happens at the end of every hour until the sixth, at which time the drummers drum, the trumpeters blow and the

<hr>

[8] A. Sayılı, *op. cit.* (1966), p. 93.

32

cymbalist plays his cymbals for a while. This occurs also at the ninth and twelfth hours.

At the beginning of the day the center of the sun will be in the appropriate degree of the Zodiac for that day on the eastern horizon, about to rise. The sun climbs until noon, then descends until nightfall.

At night the moon is seen in the Zodiacal sign and in the degree corresponding to that night and in its appropriate shape. At the beginning of the night the first of the glass roundels will show light like a nail which increases until it is filled with light. This happens until six are fully lit: then musicians do their duty as they do during the day.[9]

The second example is the famous elephant water clock from which can be told the passage of the constant hours. When the tip of the scribe's pen reaches to 7.5 degrees it means that a constant half an hour of the day elapsed, the bird whistles on the top of the cupola and rotates. The figure sitting on the balcony lifts his hand from the beak of the falcon. A ball drops from the beak of the falcon to the mouth of the serpent, which descents slowly, until its head reaches the vase on the shoulder of the elephant and the ball falls on a cymbal. Then the serpent rises to its original position.[10]

Lynn White says,

Western scholars had thought that conical valves first appeared in Leonardo's drawings, but Al-Jazarî's pictures show them. Similarly, segmental gears first clearly appear in Al-Jazarî; in the west, they emerge in Giovanni de Dondi's astronomical clock finished in 1364 ... of particular importance, also, is the first unequivocal description of metal casting in closed mould-boxes with green sand, a method not used in the West until the end of the 15th century.

He adds,

these examples and other suggest Muslim transmission of Hellenistic, Far Eastern, and indeed Muslim inventions to the West.[11]

The Seljuks paid a lot of attention to public health and set up a hospital in almost each town in parallel to the *madrasas*, and developed the surgery methods and techniques.

---

[9] Donald R. Hill, *The Book of Knowledge of Ingenious Mechanical Devices*. Boston 1974.
[10] *ibidem.*
[11] *ibidem.*

Ibn al-Nafis was born in 607 H. in Damascus, he was educated at medical college-cum-hospital founded by Nur al-Din Zangî. After finishing his school he went to Cairo where he was appointed as principal at the famous Nasrî Hospital. He also served at Masuriya School at Cairo.

He wrote several books on medicine, but the most famous one is *mujez al-qânûn*. His major original contribution of great significance was his discovery of pulmonary blood circulation. George Sarton says, in the *Introduction of the History of Science,*

> The best known of his writings is his Commentary on the Qânûn, *Kitab al-Mujiz al-qânûn.*

> Another work of Ibn al-Nafis, his commentary on the anatomical part of the *Qânûn,* the *sharh tashrih ibn Sinâ* seems to be extremely interesting from the physiological point of view. In five different places, Ibn al-Nafis quotes Ibn Sinâ's views or circulation in heart and lung and repeats the Galenic fragments included in Ibn Sinâ's account and then proceeds to contradict these views with the utmost vigour. Five times does he states in unmistakable term that the venous blood cannot pass from the right to the left ventricle through visible or invisible pores in the septum, but must pass through the venous artery to the lungs, be mingled there with air, pass through the arterial vein.[12]

Ibn al-Nafis book was translated into Latin and published in Venice in 1547. *Ebenefis philosopiae medici expositio Superquintum canonem Evicennae ab Andrea Alpago bellunensi ex arabico in latinum versa.*

Galeno's general theory of the bodily functions held its ground till Harvey discovered the circulation of the blood. In his *De humanus corporis fabrica* (1543), Andreas Vesalius expressed discreet scepticism about the pores in the inter ventricular septum. Later Realdus Columbus (1516-1580) in his *De re anatomica* (1559) presented his views on pulmonary passage and supported his observations with well-designed experiments. Also Servetius expressed that the blood mixes with air in the lungs.

---

[12] G. Sarton, *Introduction to the History of Science.* Vol. 3, Part. I.

Younus Emre et sa philosophie

Prof. Dr. İbrahim Agâh Çubukçu

Younus Emre est né en 1240 et il est mort en 1320. Il était de famille turque et il connaissait très bien la culture générale de son pays.

A l'époque où il vécût, il y avait de différentes cultures en Anatolie. La vie politique était très animée et la souffrance du peuple était très forte à cause de la guerre. Cette guerre était, d'une part, entre les turcs et les mongols, et de l'autre, entre les principautés turques.

Les turcs étaient venus massivement en Anatolie au XIème siècle. En arrivant à ce pays ils y avaient apporté leur culture essentielle de l'Asie centrale.

En Asie centrale, les *kams* (leaders religieux des chamanistes), après avoir été convertis à l'islam, étaient devenus des derviches du soufisme. En Anatolie ils s'appelaient *Ata*, *Baba* ou bien *Abdal*. L'un de ces derviches, dont le nom était Ahmed Yesevî, avait écrit des poésies pour propager l'islam en Asie centrale. Au XIIème siècle son influence était énorme. Ses disciples étaient venus en Anatolie. On croit que le *Divan-ı-Hikmet*, livre de poésie en turc, appartient à Ahmed Yesevî.

Younus Emre a été influencé par Ahmed Yesevî. Il a interprété l'islam avec une grande tolérance. D'ailleurs les turcs étaient une nation tolérante parce qu'ils connaissaient le bouddhisme, le manichéisme, le chamanisme, le judaïsme et le christianisme. A certains moments quelques tribus turques avaient accepté le bouddhisme, puis le manichéisme et d'autres religions. A partir du VIIIème siècle les turcs avaient des rapports avec les pays musulmans. Ils ont été convertis massivement à l'islam à partir du Xème siècle. Mais ils apportèrent leur coutume et leur pensée à l'islam. C'est pour cela que l'interprétation religieuse des turcs est différente de celle d'autres nations musulmanes.

En plus, en Anatolie il y avait des oeuvres d'anciennes civilisations. Surtout les hittites et les romains ont laissé beaucoup d'oeuvres monumentales.

A l'époque de Younus il y avait un grand nombre de sectes en Anatolie. Il a choisi la méthode du soufisme pour unifier leurs différentes croyances.

D'abord il a donné de l'importance à l'humanité parce que Dieu a dit dans le Coran: *Nous avons créé l'homme dans la plus belle proportion. Nous avons honoré les fils d'Adam.*

D'après Younus Emre, l'homme peut discerner l'essence de son existence. C'est pour cela qu'il a dit:

Je ne dis pas que je suis en moi, je ne suis pas en moi. Il y a quelque
essence pensante en moi-même.

Alors, en vérité, l'homme signifie une idée plus que son corps. L'homme peut apprécier le monde et qu'il peut mener une vie significative. Celui qui se connaît soi-même, respect le droit de l'homme. Chaque individu est la créature de Dieu. Ceux qui aiment Dieu, aiment aussi sa créature. A ce que Younus Emre croit, la science est d'abord d'apprendre la science, et après est de connaître soi-même. En nous connaissant, nous connaissons tout le monde. En réalité tout le monde est égal. Younus a dit à ce sujet:

Notre nom est soufis
Notre ennemi est la haine
Nous ne détestons personne
Tout le monde est égal à nos yeux.

L'homme a la clairvoyance de saisir des changements sur la terre. Il peut penser à l'existence de l'univers, aux nuances des saisons, et au but d'être créé. En plus, il peux être amoureux de Dieu. Ainsi il s'approche de Dieu. Qu'est-ce que l'homme doit faire pour s'approcher de Dieu? Les réponses en sont plusieurs.

D'abord il faut faire plaisir aux autres. Younus a dit à ce sujet:

Un vieil homme barbu ne peut savoir son attitude à la fin. Qu'il n'aille
pas à la Mecque pour le pèlerinage s'il donne quelque inquiétude au
coeur d'autrui. Le coeur est le trône de Dieu. Dieu a regardé le coeur.
Celui qui a tourmenté les sentiments du coeur est malheureux ici-bas et
dans l'au-delà. Pense aux autres, comme tu as pensé à toi-même. C'est
du sens des quatre livres célestes qu'il s'agit.

Deuxièmement, il faut aider l'humanité. Le travail pour gagner de l'argent est notre devoir. Mais il est nécessaire de voir les besoins des autres. Nous devons leur donner un coup de main. Younus a dit dans ses poésies:

Travailles, gagnes, manges, fais manger, établis d'amitiés avec un coeur.
C'est mieux que de faire le pèlerinage mille fois.

Ô *Moufti* (prédicateur) il est mieux de faire plaisir à un coeur que d'aller
au pèlerinage mille fois.

Si tu a visité un malade et que tu lui a donné un verre d'eau, la récom-
pense est comme si tu avais bu le vin du paradis à l'au-delà.

Troisièmement, l'homme doit mener une vie très honnête et très sage.
Younus a dit:

> J'ai effacé la haine de mon coeur. Celui qui nourrit la haine, il perd sa
> religion. Nous ne haïssons personne. L'ennemi est notre ami quand
> même. Le lieu où il y a de la solitude est le quartier et la ville pour nous.

La modestie et la justice sont des essentiels pour l'éthique de Younus.
Lisons ces vers de ses poésies:

> Que la voie s'allonge tout droit. Que l'oeil voit la vérité. Que l'homme
> soit modeste. En réalité l'oeil égoïste n'est pas l'oeil désirable.

Younus aime toujours la paix en disant ceci:

> Le derviche ne lève pas sa main envers celui qui le frappe. Il ne dit
> aucun mot à celui qui l'insulte. Il n'est pas fâché avec celui qui est
> méchant. Autrement tu ne peux pas être derviche.

L'homme, en purifiant son coeur et en bien dirigeant sa conduite s'approche de Dieux et l'aime.

La pensée de Younus est une philosophie de l'amour: *L'homme, était
l'esprit, avant que Dieu n'ait créé l'univers. Les esprits étaient heureux au Trône
de Dieu.* Younus a dit au sujet de l'esprit:

> Ni le ciel, ni le monde existaient
> il n'y avait aucune parole
> Les amoureux adoraient
> Le Dieu qui ne ressemble à personne.

> Avant qu'Adam n'ait été créé,
> Sans que l'Esprit n'ait été unifié avec le corps,
> Et avant même que le Satan n'ait été expulsé,
> Je voyais le ciel.

Dieu a dit aux Esprits, comme on le croyait dans l'islam: *Ne suis-je pas
votre Dieu?* Ils ont répondu en disant *oui.* Un moment après Dieu a créé l'univers
et la race de l'humanité est venue avec son corps sur la terre. Il a dit dans le
Coran: *J'ai soufflé à l'homme une étincelle de mon Esprit.* Alors l'Esprit humain
est saint, mais il est dérangé par le désir du corps. En ce cas il s'agit de deux

essentiels dans l'existence de l'homme: L'un est l'Esprit et l'autre le corps qui a besoin d'être nourri. Les exigences du corps conduisent l'homme à des ambitions. Parfois l'homme ne peut pas sortir du cercle de la causalité pour faire plaisir à ses ambitions. Tandis que l'Esprit a la nostalgie d'être heureux. Il est séparé du Trône céleste. Il est comme un étranger dans ce monde. Plus les ambitions du corps augmentent, plus il est malheureux. L'homme sait qu'il mourra un jour. Mais il est très difficile de quitter l'intérêt. Younus a dit à ce sujet:

Un jour vient et je reste sans toi
Le loup et l'oiseau me mangent
Mon corps s'épuise et je deviens comme terre
Qu'est-ce que je fais ma vie?

La prédestination courbe notre dos
Et elle ne permet pas de parler à notre langue
Je souhaite que soient sains et saufs
Ceux qui demandent de nos nouvelles en cas de maladie
Mon corps se met au stade des funérailles
On nous habille d'une chemise sans col
Je souhaite que soient sains et saufs
Ceux qui nous lavent sagement.

Younus se rappelle de la mort et il nous la rappelle. Alors il faut bien apprécier la vie. Le temps passe, mais nous l'oublions très souvent. En réalité l'homme est étranger sur la terre. Il faut sauver son esprit du mal de ce monde. Il faut le purifier pour être heureux éternellement. Mais les intérêts et les ambitions ne nous laissent pas. Le sauvetage de l'homme dépend de sa conduite. Il faut gagner la vraie vie qui est à la présence de Dieu. Ici-bas, l'homme est comme un voyageur qui doit passer un examen. Younus se plaigne de ce monde en disant:

Je ne sais pas dans quel cas je suis?
Je suis un rossignol étranger
Comment ris-je? Je suis dans le piège
Tandis que je suis venu pour chanter sur la rose.

Je suis un rossignol étranger
Je suis venu pour visiter la rose dans le vignoble
J'ai voulu me consoler et rire
Mon gémissement se répand dans le monde.

Qu'ils disent un étranger est mort
Qu'ils soient avertis trois jours après
Qu'ils lavent mon corps avec l'eau froide
Regarde, je suis un étranger.

38

Dans sa philosophie Younus nous montre la voie de la béatitude. C'est l'amour de Dieu. Si vous aimez Dieu alors il ne s'agit d'aucune peur et d'aucun sentiment de solitude. Il n'y a même aucune importance à attribuer à l'existence ou à la mort. Il a dit au sujet de l'amour de Dieu:

Je ne jouis pas de l'existence,
Je ne me plaigne pas de l'absence
Je me console de ton amour
Il me faut toi, seulement toi

Certains disent paradis, paradis
Il consiste d'une maison et de quelques fées
Donne-les à ceux qui en demandent
Il me faut toi, seulement toi.

Younus croit à la force de l'amour divin. C'est l'amour divin qui peut rendre libre l'homme éternellement. Ceux qui aiment Dieu du profond du coeur se sauvent des conditions amenant au malheur. Les esprits empêchés par des ambitions du corps ne sont pas indépendants. Plus que nous aimons Dieu, plus nous devenons indépendants spirituellement. Autrement l'homme reste malheureux ici-bas et à l'au-delà. Voyons ce que Younus a dit:

Il ne signifie rien d'arriver à ce monde
Il ne signifie rien de rire ici-bas
A la fin tu mourras
Si tu ne sens aucune étincelle de l'amour.

Alors l'amour c'est la seule essence qui nous sauve, nous rend indépendants et heureux. Younus est amoureux de Dieu. C'est pour ça qu'il a joui de la vie en se disant:

Ma langue est la langue d'oiseau
Ma province est la province d'Ami
Je suis rossignol, mon ami est rose
Savez que ma rose ne devient pas pâle.

Il faut être un oiseau qui vole
Il faut s'installer dans un faubourg
Il faut boire d'un sorbet
Qu'ils ne s'éveillent pas, ceux qui en boivent.

En résumé, Younus nous conseille d'être en paix avec nous-même, avec Dieu et avec la société, comme il a dit dans ces vers:

Venez, connaissons-nous
Rendons les affaires faciles
Aimons et soyons aimés
Le monde ne reste à personne.

Dans ses poésies, Younus Emre a défendu la liberté de conscience contre les pressions. Ses interprétations sont inspirées au Coran. Parce que Dieu y a dit: *Aucune pression sur la conscience. Veux-tu forcer des hommes pour qu'ils deviennent croyants? Ô Muhammad, tu est un rappeleur. Il ne t'est pas permis d'obliger les gens pour qu'elles croient.*

Younus, en le sachant, était respectueux de la croyance des autres gens. A l'époque où il vivait, il y avait plusieurs religions et de différentes interprétations du Coran en Anatolie. Il y avait aussi des confréries religieuses provenant de l'islam. Les mongoles étaient à peine musulmans. Certains d'entre eux étaient païens. Dans cette situation les poésies de Younus ont influencé les partisans d'autres croyances. Parce que Younus disait:

> Si tu as une fois tourmenté un coeur, ta prière n'est pas valable. Ne crois pas que soixante-douze peuples ne fassent pas des prières.

Younus, en ne s'éloignant pas de la coutume turque, respectait d'autres croyances et il racontait l'islam d'une manière aimable. En réalité il était humaniste. Mais son humanisme était différent de celui du stoïcisme, ou bien de celui du marxisme. Parce qu'il croyait en un seul Dieu. Dans ses poésies il interprétait le Coran d'après sa philosophie. Il y reflétait l'art turc, la coutume turque et l'esprit turc en écrivant en turc. Mais, de l'autre côté, il ne faisait pas de différence entre les gens. Il disait que tout le monde avait été créé par Dieu. Puisque nous aimons Dieu, nous devons aimer ses créatures. La crainte qui pèse sur la conscience vexe les gens. Alors il faut que les gens de n'importe quelle religion, s'entendent et vivent dans la paix. Il n'attestait pas les interprétations fanatiques de l'islam. Au lieu de cela il présentait une méthode basée sur l'amour. C'est pour cela qu'il est réussi à rassembler de différentes gens sous ses pensées philosophiques. Il disait dans ses poésies:

> L'amour est prédicateur pour nous, le coeur est la communauté
> Le visage de l'Ami est le lieu saint pour s'orienter
> Et la prière existe toujours
> Aussitôt que nous avons vu le visage de l'ami, le polythéisme s'est épuisé
> C'est pour ça que la loi religieuse est restée au-dehors de la porte.

> La vérité est une mer et la loi religieuse est un bateau
> Beaucoup de gens ne sont pas sorties du bateau et n'ont pas plongé dans la mer.

> Si quelqu'un ne regarde pas aux soixante-douze peuples avec le même oeil et qu'il est saint en *shariat* (la loi religieuse), en vérité il est révoltant.

> La loi religieuse et la confrérie religieuse sont des voies pour celui qui les préfère. Mais la vérité et le sens ésotérique sont plus profonds.

Finalement, je peux dire que d'après Younus, l'homme reçoit la vérité avec l'amour. L'Amour est une méthode de partager la beauté de la vie. L'Amour est la paix avec soi-même et avec d'autres personnes. C'est pour cela qu'il nous a dit:

Younus Emre dit ô prédicateur! Si tu a fait mille fois le pèlerinage, ce n'est pas suffisant.
Il vaut mieux de faire plaisir à un coeur.

Islam and Christian Spirituality in Spain:
Contacts, Influences, Similarities

Prof. Dr Francisco de Borja de Medina, S.J.

The theme assigned to me is so vast that it is impossible to deal with it in a paper that must necessarily be brief. I only propose to set forth the state of the question of a possible relationship between the spiritual aspects present in two apparently antagonistic cultures: Islam and Christianity. This relationship, accepted by the majority of scholars, with regard to its basic points, is greatly discussed as far as its extent and its particular details.

I will first briefly mention some fundamental features of the historical context in which this cultural intercommunication between Christian and Muslim Spain developed, so that I can then list the possible mutual influences, among which is spirituality. Finally, I will make clear the state of the question, giving special attention to two special cases that are of greater interest to scholars: the Spanish mystics, the reformers of the Carmelite Order, St. Teresa and St. John of the Cross.

The nine centuries of living together, or if we wish, existing together, of the three cultures – Christian, Jewish, and Muslim – could do no less than put its brand on all levels of Spanish life, also on the spiritual experiences in their widest spectrum. I have said nine centuries, because I count up to 1606-1614, when the expulsion of the Moriscos took place, the great majority of whom – it was no secret – were either crypto-Muslims or openly practising Muslims.

A symbol of this living together in the thirteenth century could be the epitaph of Ferdinand III of Castile (St. Ferdinand), conqueror of the three Muslim kingdoms watered by the Guadalquivir – Córdoba, Jaen, Seville – assisted by the Nasri king of Granada.

Ferdinand died in Seville in 1248. His tomb is in the cathedral's Royal Chapel: there are four marble tablets, two on each of its two sides; the inscription is in Latin and Castilian on the right side, and Arabic and Hebrew on the left. The inscription's author is Alfonso X, known as «The Wise», Ferdinand's son and successor.

The text is basically the same, but each language uses its own way of dating Ferdinand's death: the year of the Incarnation (the last day of May 1252); of the Spanish Era (the last day of May 1290); the year of the Hegira (Friday night, the 21st day of the month Rabi° I, in the year 650); the year of the Creation of the World (Friday night, 22nd day of the month Siwan, in the year 5012).

In the three vernacular versions, there is suppressed the phrase from the Latin version, which refers to the conquest of Seville as a Christian re-conquest, since this can offend the susceptibilities of the other religions: *de manibus eripuit paganorum et cultui restituit christiano* [he took Seville from the hands of the heathen and restored it to Christian cult].

There is also suppressed the Christian formula of describing death: *ubi solvens naturae debitum ad Dominum transmigravit* [where, (in Seville), he paid the debt due to nature and transmigrated to the Lord].

The Arabic and Hebrew inscriptions introduce the invocations proper to each religion. In Arabic: *May Allah take pleasure in him* and *May Allah have mercy on him*. In Hebrew: *May his soul be in the Garden of Eden*. The Castilian uses no special formula.

Each language in the epitaph uses its vernacular equivalent for the Latin Hispania, the land common to the three: España, Al-Andalus, Sefarad. It is because of this that Spanish Jews are called the Sephardim, and the Muslims, Andalusians. This is the name that we use for Spanish Muslims [in Spanish, Andalusíes].

The deceased king's virtues are exalted one by one in a way that could be accepted by all:

> Here lies the king most honoured, Don Fernando, Lord of Castile and of Toledo, of Leon, of Gallecia, of Seville, of Córdoba, of Murcia and of Iahen, he who conquered all of Spain, the most loyal, the most truthful, the most generous, the most valiant, the most handsome, the most gallant, the most patient – here the Arabic introduces three new attributes: the most merciful, the most clement, the most compassionate –, the most humble, the most pious, he who served God the most, who weakened and destroyed all his enemies, who raised up and honoured all his friends.

44

One of these friends had been the Muslim Lord of Arjona, Muḥammad Ibn Yūsuf Ibn Naṣr Ibn al-Aḥmar, whom Ferdinand helped to obtain and keep the kingdom of Granada, and offered his protection, naturally, in exchange for vassalage. This included, besides «tributum», paying a tribute, «auxilium» and «consilium» that is to say, providing the king of Castile with military assistance and counselling in state matters when asked.

In 1310, the king of Granada confirms a Royal Writ by Ferdinand IV, as "Don Nazar, king of Granada, vassal of the King." In another document, he entitles himself in the style of the kings of Castile: "Don Nazar, by the grace of God, king of Granada, of Málaga, of Almería, of Ronda, of Guadix and Amir Amuminin." [sic] About 1360, Pedro I of Castile (1350-1369) conferred the Order of the Band on his vassal King Muḥammad V of Granada (1354-1391). The Order's coat of arms profusely decorates the Lion's Quarter in the Alhambra, as it does in the contemporary Alcazar of King Don Pedro in Seville, built by Granadine architects sent by Muḥammad.

So the Islamic kingdom of Granada, notwithstanding its recurrent clashes with its Christian neighbours, included Castile, could last for more than two an a half centuries and have a share in the political and military affairs of Al-Andalus-Hispania, as one of the five peninsular kingdoms, the others being the Christian kingdoms of Castile, Aragón, Portugal and Navarre.

Christian communities, known as «Mozarabic» [arabized], coexisted in the lands under Islam, as did Islamic communities, the «Mudejar», in Christian kingdoms. In the same way, there were conversions on both sides. There were «muladi» in the lands under Muslim control and «tornadizos» in Christian kingdoms. Jewish communities lived in both lands and there were conversions from this religion to either of the two. The Jews were also arabized.

This tolerance, notwithstanding its tensions and difficulties, was still officially recognized in the thirteenth century by Alfonso X in his Seven «Partidas», or «Parts», the general law of Castile.

Alfonso's legislation does not renounce attracting others to one's own faith, this is common to both religions; but this attraction is left within a perspective of personal freedom. Partida VII, title XXV, law II, reads:

> Through good words and convenient preaching, Christians ought to work to convert the Moors to make them believe in our faith, and to lead them to it, and not by force, nor by pressure; because if the will of Our Lord were to lead them to it, and to make them believe by force, he would pressure them, if he wished, because he has complete power to do it. But he is not pleased with a service that comes from fear, but a service that

is given willingly and without pressure. Since he does not want to pressure them, nor use force, so we also forbid anyone to pressure them or to use force on them in this regard.

In the Castilian King's policy of toleration, actually inspired by God's way of acting, some see an influence of the Koran with regard to the people of the Book (*ahl-al-Kitāb*).

But it is significant that, a century earlier, African invaders, the Almoravids and, above all, the Almohads, introduced intolerance in Al-Andalus. In 1147, the Almohad calif, Abu Muḥammad ʿAbd al-Mu'min, al-Qa'im, ordered all Jews and Christians to be converted to Islam under death penalty. They fled to Christian lands. A similar policy of intolerance will take place in Castile and Aragón during the 15th century, until the tragic alternative – conversion to Christianity or expulsion – was enforced by royal power, first with regard to the Jews in 1492 and later the Muslims in three stages: 1499-1501 with those living in the kingdom of Granada, in 1502 with the Mudejar in the crown of Castile, and 1525 with those in the crown of Aragón.

This radical change of attitude is reflected in the sepulchral epitaph of the Catholic Kings, Ferdinand and Isabella, in the Royal Chapel in Granada's cathedral. It is diametrically opposed to that of St. Ferdinand in Seville. Written in a single language, in Latin, and without any eulogy except their repressive action against Islam and Judaism, it says:

> Mahometice secte postratores et heretice pervicacie extintores Fernandus Aragonum et Helisabetha Castelle vir et uxor unanimes Catolice appellati marmoreo clauduntur hoc tumulo.
> [Ferdinand of Aragón and Isabella of Castile, husband and wife, whom everyone calls Catholic, who wiped out the Muslim sects and made the heretical stubbornness [Judaism] extinct, are enclosed in this marble tomb.]

As far as mutual personal relations during the long periods of peace or truce, Christians and Muslims visited each other, engaged in business, intermarried, their kings assisted each other in their respective civil wars, and during turbulent times they sought refuge in each other's land.

Al-Andalus became soon a most important cultural center in Europe and at the same time the bridge between the Islamic East and the Christian West. The brilliant civilization in Córdoba, inaugurated by the Ummayyad dynasty, in the 8th century, attracted Christians from the peninsular kingdoms, and these were influenced by Islamic art, vocabulary, military and judicial organization, sciences and philosophy, literature, etc. When the caliphate of Córdoba was dissolved and dismembered, culture continued in the Taifa kingdoms during the 11th and 12th centuries, and passed into the Court of Castile.

Toledo, the capital of the Visigothic Kingdom, re-occupied in 1085 by Alfonso VI, became the most important center for irradiating Islamic culture to the Peninsula and Europe. He married Zaida, daughter-in-law of the ᶜabbādi King of Seville al-Muᶜtamid, was surrounded by Muslim and Jewish scholars, dressed in Arabic fashion, his court was like a Muslim court and took the title of «Emperor of the two religions». Even Mozarabic clerics from Toledo used Arabic names, spoke in Arabic, and knew little latin. Later on, his grandson Alfonso VII was acknowledged as the Emperor of the three religions, and when he entered a city, was welcome and accompanied in procession by the three communities: the Christians carrying the pallium and a Cross, the Muslims the Koran and the Jews the Torah. In Aragón, King Pedro I (1094-1104) signed royal documents in Arabic as Pedro ben Sancho.

Through the so-called school of translators in Toledo, set up during the reign of Alfonso VII by the archbishop Don Raymundo, Europe came to know the most famous Arabic scientific works: mathematics, astronomy, medicine, alchemy, physics, natural history, philosophy, metaphysics, psychology, logic, ethics and political theory, as well as the glosses by Arabic philosophers on Greco-Latin works.

Two centuries later, with Alfonso X (1252-1284), Eastern Arabic science entered the West, together with the Al-Andalus cultural treasures of the 11th and 12th centuries. The king gathered around him Muslims, Jews, and Mozarabs, systematized the work of translation in Toledo and used the Castilian language as a vehicle of culture. The translations were done by a team of al-fuqahā', rabbis, and clerics. They translated the Koran, the works of Algazel, Avicenna, Averroes, etc. Among the works translated into Castilian were *Kalila wa Dimna*, a collection of Eastern fables, and the *Escala de Mahoma* (the Miᶜraj, or Ascension of Mohammed), the Prophet's nocturnal voyage (Sura 17, v 1). This was then translated from Castilian into Latin and French and influenced Dante's *Divina Commedia*. Scholars from all over Europe came to Toledo to help with translations.

Alfonso established in Seville a Studium Generale of Latin and Arabic for the study of the sciences, and entrusted Muḥammad el Ricoti with directing a school in Murcia for teaching Muslims, Jews, and Christians.

In the last quarter of the 18th century, the ex-Jesuit Juan Andrés, an exile in Italy, in his encyclopedic work *Dell'origine, progressi e stato attuale d'ogni letteratura* (7 vols. 1782-1799) gives a glimpse of what medieval European culture owes to the Spanish Arabs. His work, often reprinted in Italy, was quickly translated into Spanish, French, and German. In literature, he defended the Arabic origin of rhyme and of the meter of the troubadours, which was the same as advocating the same origin for all European poetry than considers Provençal poetry as its immediate predecessor.

But this is only the formal aspect of our topic. The coexistence of the three cultures for almost a thousand years influenced the shaping of Spain and its very being. This obvious fact unchained heated polemics at the time of determining and measuring the contribution that each of these cultures brought to the formation of Spain.

This polemic is still with us; it was brought on by the work of Américo Castro, *España en su historia. Cristianos, moros y judíos* (Buenos Aires, 1948), and took on a wider aspect when Claudio Sánchez Albornoz entered the picture with his *España un enigma histórico* (Buenos Aires, 1956).

Castro's thesis, recast in his *La realidad histórica de España* (México, 1954), many times reprinted (7th ed. 1980), gives the primacy to Islamic influence in the Spanish tissue in all levels of life. For him the Spaniards did not begin to exist until the Arabic invasion of 711. In practice he denies any contribution on the part of the Roman-Visigoths. Assigns to the Jews a main contribution in the formation of Castilian literature and, from the 15th century, an influence on the several aspects of the religious life, which will continue through the conversi in the 16th century. These conversi are, according to Castro, those who put in motion Castile's spiritual renewal.

Castro's statements give rise to most varied positions, from total refusal to more complete acceptance. This was more general among scholars of literature than among historians. The positions became polarized. The critics gathered around one or the other extreme. Ramón Menéndez Pidal, Emilio García Gómez, Leo Spitzer, Marcel Bataillon, among others, entered the field, either opposing or correcting Castro's radical views. José Luis Gómez Martínez has studied the vicissitudes of the polemic in *Américo Castro y el origen de los españoles: historia de una polémica* (Madrid, 1975).

It has been stated that Castro's approach has constituted the most complex and systematic attempt to analyze the Hispanic past in a crucial era of its formation. But, as Marcel Bataillon pointed out, Castro made history vertical, cutting through the strata of Hispanic-Muslim events, but neglected the horizontal history of Spanish-European relationships. Ortega y Gasset showed that the

Germanic element – the Goths – was the basic element to the forming of Spanish history and character. And Sánchez Albornoz insisted on the Christian kingdom of Leon, heir of the Roman-Visigothic kingdom as the essential factor in the making of the character of Spanish history and people. This kingdom would displace Islam and re-populate with its Christian subjects the greater part of the lands of Al-Andalus abandoned by the Muslims.

Through other ways, a few years before Castro's polemical work, Miguel Asín Palacios pointed out, in his studies of the Islamic mystical authors from Al-Andalus, the analogy of doctrine and language of the Ṣūfī masters of the 12th century with the Christian Spanish Mystics of the 16th century, and in particular, with the reformers of the Carmelite Order, St. Teresa and St. John of the Cross.

According to Asín, the mysticism of Al-Andalus had developed, with its own sensibility, the doctrines and methods of Eastern Ṣūfism, and gave birth to a school of its own. The first master, with some originality, was Ibn Masarra, from the 10th century, to whom Asín dedicated a work in 1914, *Abenmasarra y su escuela*. Ibn Masarra's teaching, transmitted by his disciples, constituted the doctrinal basis of the mysticism of Al-Andalus.

One of those who received inspiration, in part, from this school is Ibn ᶜArabī of Murcia (d. 1240). Asín wrote four articles on his life and work, in the *Boletín de la Real Academia de la Historia* (between 1925-1928), anticipating his larger study *El Islam cristianizado. Estudio del sufismo a través de las obras de Abenarabi de Murcia* (Madrid, 1931). The title itself indicates the thesis's slant. In contrast with Louis Massignon, who defends the autonomous origin of Ṣūfism in *Essai sur les origines du lexique tecnique de la mystique musulmane* (Paris, 1922), Asín bases the resemblances on «cultural restitution.» Using his words:

> Islam offers itself ... under a double aspect: on the one hand it transmits the classical and Christian legacy of the East to Europe, and on the other increases this treasure by its own inventive effort, because the borrowings that the Eastern hand had taken from the Hellenic and Patristic treasures are later returned, with increment, to the Christian creditors of the west.

Thus, in 1916, as the fruit of his research on the possible Christian influences on Islamic mysticism, Asín has published in *Patrologia Orientalis* (XIII, 3. Paris, 1916), *Logia et Agrapha D. Jesu*, in which he gathered 233 texts from Muslim spiritual writers on the sayings and deeds attributed to Jesus.

And also, in 1919, in *La Escatología musulmana en la Divina Comedia*, he had stressed the borrowings from Islam in Dante's masterpiece, as well as biblical and gospel sources from Islamic teachings on life after death.

In similar way, Ṣūfī spirituality might have, in part, its remote origin in the Christian monasticism of the East and in the desert anchorites. Asín explains this in his extended work, in three volumes, *La espiritualidad de Algazel y su sentido cristiano*, (1934-1940). These two currents are in evidence in Islam: orthodoxy represented by Algazel, and heterodoxy, in which Ibn ᶜArabī of Murcia would share. The analogies with Spanish mystics would result from this Christian origin, in both its aspects.

In *El Islam cristianizado* Asín examines, among other aspects, the spiritual doctrine and the method of Ibn ᶜArabī of Murcia and points out its coincidences with the Spanish spiritual writers of the 16th century. Thus, among the means to attain perfection, he cites, for example, the examination of conscience and the presence of God. The examen of Christian monastic origin is brought to perfection in Islam by Algazel and Ibn ᶜArabī. Asín finds resemblances in St. Ignatius of Loyola's method in the Exercises. As to the presence of God, the similarities would be found in St. Teresa and St. John of the Cross.

Asín also studied, in *Un precursor hispano-musulmán de San Juan de la Cruz*, the influence of Islamic mysticism in the reformer of Carmel through the other Al-Andalus mystic Ibn ᶜAbbād of Ronda (d. 1389). Published in *Al-Andalus* in 1933 and then printed in *Huella del Islam* (1941), a compilation of studies on Islamic influence on Christian authors, Asín reviews the Ibn ᶜAbbād of Ronda's doctrine explained in his *Commentary on the "Sentences of Ibn ᶜAṭā' Allāh of Alexandria"*, on renouncing the charisms, the love of trials, the symbol of night, etc., and analyzes his analogies with the thematic of the *Noche Oscura* (the Dark night of the spirit) in St. John of the Cross. Asín thinks that the similarities are so evident that they cannot be explained by simple coincidence or functional parallelism born of one and the same psychological-spiritual experience.

In tracing the possible channels of transmission, Asín proposes an attractive hypothesis: the influence of the masters of Muslim spirituality, through the Moriscos, on the heterodox and orthodox Spanish mystics of the 16th century.

The Moriscos were the Mudejars baptized under the threat of expulsion, the great majority of the Moriscos kept the Islamic faith and practices. These would have been, at least, in contact with the Sadili in Tunis, where the Al-Andalus spiritual tradition was preserved.

Asín continues this theme in a series of posthumous articles in *Al-Andalus*, from 1944 to 1951, recently compiled and edited, with an introduction, by the Puerto Rican Hispanist Luce López-Baralt, *Šāḍilīes y alumbrados* (Madrid, 1990). Asín also touches on the problem of the «heterodox» mystics, who appeared in Spain during the 16th century, called «alumbrados». He sees their roots in the great Šāḍilī masters. He treats, among other aspects, prayer mental and vocal, prayer of «recogimiento» and «quietud», contemplation in Molinos, the symbol of the castle or mansions of St. Teresa, and so on. His work, unfinished because of death, constitutes one of the most significant contributions to the study of comparative mysticism of this century in Spain.

As to the hypothesis of «cultural restitution», also called «Arabist theory», it has been opening its way through the difficulties and opponents, among them the above-mentioned Massignon. Helmut Hatzfeld, in *Estudios literarios sobre mística española* (Madrid, 1955), reviews the surprise and the opposition that Asín's thesis caused at the beginning. He states that even if every element of Christian Spanish mysticism is not of Arabic origin, you have to keep them in mind, when attempting to establish the sources and the models for this same mysticism.

The same year Asín's *Islam cristianizado* appeared, Angel González Palencia, in his discourse on the occasion of his becoming member of the Real Academia de la Historia (31 May 1931), starting with Juan de Andrés's hints on Islam influences in the West, went through all fields of knowledge, in which Europe and Spain were indebted to Islam. He echoes Asín's thesis on Islam's influence on Christian Spanish mysticism. This discourse and his later conference at the University of Granada in 1937, *Huellas Islámicas en el carácter español*, mark a milestone in the understanding of Islamic influences on the cultural shaping of Spain. In the appendix of his *Huellas Islámicas*, he lists the 15th and 16th century Latin editions of 60 Arabic authors, published in Europe. Both works, together with others related to this subject, were published in *Moros y Cristianos en España Medieval* in 1945, three years before Américo Castro opens the polemic with his *España en su historia*.

Claudio Sánchez Albornoz, who was pleased with and attracted to Asín's thesis, summarized it and made its own in *La España musulmana* (1946, 1986), but insisting on and perhaps over-simplifying the Christian influence on Islam. This supported his point of view in his polemic with Castro.

Sánchez Albornoz states:

> Islam, soon underwent a deep influence from Christianity. The attitude of many Ṣūfīs of the Šādilī school was profoundly Christian. One must search for the origin of their mystical position in the Pauline doctrine of the Fathers of the desert and of Eastern monasticism.
>
> In the 15th century an Al-Andalus mystic, Ibn ʿAbbād of Ronda (d. 1394) wrote 'Commentaries on the Sentences of Ibn ʿAṭāʾ Allāh of Alexandria'. In the Rondi's mysticism there appears a table of preferences and a lexicon, analogous to those that St. John of the Cross would write, and the same renunciation of charisms or divine favours and the same love for trials found in the Carmelite mystics.
>
> These striking coincidences have permitted Asín to establish the link between the two Hispanic contemplative groups: between the Muslim of the 14th and 15th centuries and the Christian of the 16th century.

So far Sánchez Albornoz.

This hypothesis, as we indicated above, and explained more unilaterally because of its excessive simplification, contradicts the thesis defended by Louis Massignon on the autonomous origin of Ṣūfīsm. Massignon states, in his study on the founder of Ṣūfīsm, *La passion de Husayn Ibn Mansûr Hallâj, martyr mystique de l'Islam* (Paris, 1922, 1975), that Muslim mysticism is based on the Koran and there is no need to refer to other outside sources. He admits the absorption by Islam of people coming from Christianity, Judaism or Mazdaism, but denies that we should resort to any influence of these in order to explain Ṣūfī doctrine and experience.

The Jesuit Paul Nwyia confirms this position in his analysis of other Ṣūfī writings.

The previously mentioned Luce López Baralt, has recently dedicated several works to the study of the Islamic influences on poetic expression and on the symbology of the mysticism of the reformer of Carmel in *San Juan de la Cruz y el Islam* (México, 1985; Madrid, 1990). Contemporary to this work is her essay, with a wither range, *Huellas del Islam en la literatura española* Madrid, 1985, 1989). Her studies treat the themes of wine and mystical inebriation, the dark night, the living flame of love, water and the fountain, ascent of the mountain, the solitary bird, etc., to which she adds the interior castle, or mansions of St. Teresa.

In the authorship of the anonymous sonnet *No me mueve mi Dios para quererte* [in the Latin version *O Deus, ego amo te*] she is inclined to see a dependence on Rābiᶜa al-ᶜAdawiyya of Baṣra (d. ca. 801), who introduced the theme of pure love among the Ṣūfī.

The author studies the possible channels of transmission or intermediate sources of inspiration for St. John of the Cross and St. Teresa. One of the channels could be European mystical literature, influenced, in its turn, during the Middle Ages by Islamic authors, such as Algazel and Avicenna. But the resemblances, in the cases studied, would be nearer the original Islamic source. On the other hand, she admits the possible influence of Jewish exegesis on St. John of the Cross. In any case she recognizes that, notwithstanding the obvious resemblances, the lost link has not yet been found.

Paul Nwyia is very cautious in accepting Ṣūfī or Šāḍilī influence on St. John of the Cross, and particularly from Ibn ᶜAbbād. In his article "Ibn ᶜAbbād de Ronda et Jean de la Croix", which appeared in *Al-Andalus* in 1957, Nwyia reviews Asín's statements on this point, in particular with regard to the terminology of «anchura» (*basṭ*) [comfort] and «apretura» (*qabḍ*) [trouble] (consolation-desolation), and the underlying doctrine, the symbol of the night and the renunciation of all charisms.

Nwyia thinks that the texts by the Rondi adduced are very interesting, but out of their semantic context they lose their value as models and would indicate resemblances rather than dependence.

Massignon had shown the same reserve in "Textes musulmans pouvant concerner la nuit de l'ésprit", *Études Carmélitaines* (October 1938). As to the channel of transmission, Nwyia does not reject the Asín hypothesis on the Morisco milieu, but proposes, as does Jean Baruzi, whom Nwyia quotes, that before coming to any conclusion a serious study of that milieu and possible contact of St. John of the Cross with it, should be done.

Recent studies have dealt with the new-Christian origin of St. John of the Cross, supposing him of Jewish and Morisco descent, and so close to the Morisco milieu on the part of his mother Catalina Alvarez. But this double origin has not been proven, (see, for example, José Gómez-Menor Fuentes, *El linaje familiar de Sta. Teresa y de S. Juan de la Cruz*. Toledo, 1970), nor has the hypothesis of the knowledge among the Moriscos of the Šāḍilī doctrine, which is akin to that of Ibn ᶜAbbād and his disciples, been confirmed.

As López-Baralt shows, the many recent works on Morisco «Aljamiado» texts (that is to say, texts in Castilian written with Arabic characters) do not corroborate, up to now, Asín's hypothesis. The Morisco contemporary to the Spanish spiritual authors seem not to know the Islamic mystical literature of their Al-Andalus predecessors.

On the other side, the direct influence of Islamic spirituality on other Christian authors cannot be denied. Juan Vernet, for example, in his recent work, *Ce que la culture doit aux Arabes d'Espagne* (1985), treats, among other themes, Islam's influence on the Franciscan Ramon Llull (1231-1315).This is the thesis already defended by Julián Ribera in 1899, "Orígenes de la filosofía de Raimundo Lulio", (in *Homenaje a Menéndez y Pelayo* II) and by Asín, on the same occasion, in his work "Mohidin" (Ibid.) and, years later, in the already mentioned *Abenmasarra y su escuela*. Asín undervalues this influence in "El lulismo exagerado" (*Cultura Española* 1 [1906] 533-541). But others do not doubt the importance of Ṣūfī influence on Llull and from him on the late-medieval Christian mysticism and even afterwards.

Llull knew Arabic and wrote some of his works in Arabic. He promoted the foundation of schools of Eastern studies in Europe and chairs of Arabic in European universities. Through his personal reading, his direct sources of inspiration are the Al-Andalus mystics, in particular Ibn ᶜArabī of Murcia. Of Islamic dependence are *Els cent noms de Deu*, *Llibre de les besties*, the autobiographical novel *Blanquerna*, *El llibre d'amic e d'amat*. He wrote this last work, as he himself states in Blanquerna, following the Ṣūfī method. In his book, *Oracions de Ramon*, he incorporates Islamic ideas on mental prayer.

The influence of Llull on the Franciscan school was so notable, that the Franciscan Order established chairs of Lullism in its own University Colleges. His thinking passed into the Franciscan spiritual authors of the 16th century, such as Francisco de Osuna in his *Tercer abecedario espiritual*, whose influence on St. Teresa is normally admitted.

To conclude, a word on the Lead books of the Sacro Monte of Granada. They are the touchstone for proving both the ignorance of Islamic culture in the Spanish theologians of the 16th and 17th centuries, and the ambiguous religious language of their counterfeiters, with all probability two Granada Moriscos: Alonso del Castillo and Miguel de Luna.

Ignacio de las Casas, a Morisco Jesuit from Granada, whose mother tongue was Arabic and was familiar with Islam, discovered the fraud by recognizing in the Lead books Islamic thinking based on the Koran and on other traditions, which circulated among the Moriscos, such as *Escala de Mahoma* Miʿraj, already mentioned.

Among the several theologians who accepted the books as documents of apostolic origin from the 1st century, there were 20 from the Society of Jesus and these were among the best known. The theologians found in the books clear proof of the coming of St. James to Spain, the tradition of the Assumption of Mary, the doctrine of her Immaculate Conception and one of the most ancient Trinitarian formulas. But this formula – Only God is God, Jesus Spirit of God –, as Casas had shown, was Islamic.

Enough with this review to situate the state of the question. In resuming we can say:

1. The coexistence of the three cultures in Spain for almost a millennium, could not but influence and leave its mark on its history and character.

2. One of these fundamental aspects is the Al-Andalus Muslim spirituality, in particular, Ṣūfīsm and Šāḍilīsm.

3. This spirituality is expressed with a vocabulary and a symbology which offers extraordinary analogies with the Christian spiritual authors of the 16th century.

4. This is seen, especially, in the two great figures of the Carmelite reform: St. Teresa and St. John of the Cross.

5. Nevertheless, until now the channel of transmission has not been traced.
   a) The theory of «cultural restitution», which is based on a supposed influence of Christianity on Islamic mysticism and of this on Christian mysticism, does not satisfy all.
   b) Given the close analogies of language and symbol of St. Teresa and St. John of the Cross with the Al-Andalus mystics, the thesis of indirect transmission through Christian medieval schools of spirituality, such as the Franciscan-Llullian school, influenced by some aspects of Ṣūfīsm, is far from satisfying.
   c) On the other hand, the hypothesis of the preservation of Ṣūfī and Šāḍilī teachings and practices in the Morisco community has yet to be verified.

6. While we have not found the «missing link», we should content ourselves with noticing the existence of parallelisms and similarities which, according to another hypothesis, could have an autonomous origin, not by direct influence,

but by similar spiritual experiences in a given historical context which was marked by Islamic culture through the centuries.

a) These experiences, realized in a vital environment, equal or similar, would be expressed in an imaginative language and a symbology taken from the surrounding ambience, part of which are the sacred books that contain these obvious parallelisms. Enough to have lived in the same Al-Andalus regions in which the Muslim mystics lived, to share, at least, in the aesthetic aspect of the same experiences and to express them in a very similar imaginative and symbolic language.

b) Finally, as regards profoundly mystical religious experience, we dare to confess that as they are based on the faith in one transcendent God, common to both religions, who is near us, and who is free to communicate Himself through his gifts to believers who seek Him with a sincere heart.

Yunus Emre: l'homme, le monde et l'univers chez Yunus Emre

Prof. Dr. Kenan Gürsoy

C'est au XIIIème siècle, en Anatolie, que se déroulent la vie et l'oeuvre de Yunus Emre. Mais l'importance littéraire, philosophique, sociale et même spirituelle de ce poète et penseur, le plus aimé par le peuple turc, transcende son époque et s'étend, au fil des siècles, jusqu'à nos jours. Les derviches se sont inspirés de sa personnalité légendaire. La société d'expression turque, influencée par sa vision du monde, se reconnaît dans ses idées parfaitement intelligibles grâce à la grande simplicité de leur tournure. Enfin, la sentimentalité profonde et la commune expérience spirituelle de tout un peuple ont trouvé un sens ultime dans l'amour de Yunus pour l'univers entier et son Créateur.

En général on pense que le mystique est celui qui, se plaçant à l'écart de la société, aspire à la perfection spirituelle par une recherche intime et profonde. Yunus, lui, ne tendait pas seulement vers le plus profond de son moi intérieur, mais il était également concerné par l'autre et il s'y vouait entièrement. Pour bien comprendre cela, il nous faut un instant nous replacer dans le contexte social de l'Anatolie du XIIIème siècle, déchirée qu'elle était par les luttes politiques et les mouvements hétérodoxes. Un intense besoin de paix s'y faisait sentir et il semblait naturel, pour y parvenir, de recourir aux personnalités soufi. Yunus ne pouvait pas rester indifférent à ces problèmes: il devait, pour ainsi dire, remplir les fonctions du médecin guérissant les plaies de la communauté. L. Massignon voyait dans le soufisme

> une thérapeutique que le médecin traitant a d'abord expérimenté en soi-même afin d'en faire profiter les autres. [1]

Yunus était donc l'un d'entre eux, qui a su reconstituer, tout en lui insufflant vie, l'ordre spirituel, pilier de l'ordre social.

---

[1] Louis Massignon, *Essai sur le origines du lexique technique de la mystique musulmane*, p. 17. Paris 1954.

Ainsi apparaît le premier aspect intrinsèque à l'humanisme de Yunus: le sens social qui pourrait se résumer comme assomption de responsabilité envers l'homme. Mais il existe un autre aspect qui se dégage de cet humanisme et qui se manifeste sur le plan métaphysique. C'est à l'analyse de ce dernier – sur lequel d'ailleurs se fonde le premier – qu'est consacrée la présente étude.

Il faut admettre d'ores et déjà que, dans cette entreprise, l'issue se trouvera altérée par une difficulté fondamentale: l'élucidation ne peut s'effectuer que dans le cadre du discours philosophique, lequel est, à son tour, limité par la parole.

S'agissant chez Yunus d'une expérience spirituelle et religieuse, la parole, véhicule de connaissance positive, se révèle expression insuffisante tandis que la conceptualisation et la systématisation philosophique ne peuvent en aucun cas rendre compte d'une expérience vécue en profondeur. Néanmoins, la réalisation de cette tâche est à notre avis nécessaire pour bien situer, dans l'histoire des idées, la pensée de Yunus et pour bien saisir le sens de son éthique.

Dans l'oeuvre de Yunus Emre, le concept de l'homme ne se trouve jamais confiné en lui-même. Il est, au contraire, toujours en corrélation avec les concepts de Dieu et de l'univers. Il nous faut donc comprendre la place de l'homme dans la création; autrement dit, répondre à la question suivante: pourquoi l'homme a-t-il été créé?

Il semble que chez Yunus, comme dans le soufisme en général, l'homme occupe la place la plus importante, car toute création divine prend sa valeur par rapport à lui. Il a été créé à partir du point où sont rassemblés tous les êtres de la Terre. Cela signifie deux choses: d'une part, l'homme est la nature synthétique de la création et, de l'autre, il a une aptitude à embrasser les vérités essentielles. Ainsi que le disait Titus Burchardt,

> la nature primordiale de l'homme est comme l'aboutissement symbolique et, en quelque sorte, la source apparente de toutes les essences divines immanentes au monde.[2]

L'homme est donc le couronnement et l'unité de tout ce qui existe.

---

[2] Titus Burchardt, *Introduction aux doctrines ésotériques de l'Islam*, p. 107, Paris-Dervy - Livres, 1969.

Cette élévation de l'homme doit nous rappeler le célèbre verset coranique:

> En vérité, nous avons proposé le dépôt (de nos secrets) aux cieux et à la terre et aux montagnes, mais ils refusèrent de le porter. Mais l'homme accepta. Mais il s'est montré injuste et ignorant.[3]

L'homme est donc la seule créature qui accepte «le dépôt divin» (*amā nah*), c'est-à-dire la seule qui puisse assumer cette tâche grandiose: être investi du pouvoir de parvenir aux secrets divins. En d'autres termes, cela n'est autre chose que la potentialité de parvenir à l'essence divine (*Dhāt*).

Ainsi pouvons-nous nous représenter l'idée de dignité humaine sur laquelle Yunus a fondé son humanisme. Par ailleurs, il faut garder à l'esprit le sens idéal de cet humanisme. Car cette signification que nous donnons à la nature humaine n'est que «virtuellement» présente chez l'homme ordinaire. Elle ne devient «actuelle» que chez lui qui a effectivement réalisé toutes les «Vérités Universelles». Aussi ce dernier s'identifie à l'«Homme Universel» (ou l'Homme Parfait: *al insān al kāmil*).

L'Homme «Universel» représente celui qui est parvenu à sa pleine stature spirituelle, à sa pleine nature d'homme: soit l'homme qui a rejoint la plénitude transmise par Dieu, à travers la réception du «dépôt divin». Et c'est en atteignant cette dimension supérieure que nous comprenons le sens profond du hadith «Dieu créa l'homme à sa propre Forme».

Qui sont ces Homme(s) Parfait(s)? Ce sont les Envoyés de Dieu, les Prophètes, les Saints que nous rencontrons tout au long de l'histoire des religions monothéistes. Car en effet, la pensée de Yunus, comme celle de l'Islam, ne fait pas de distinction entre les différents Envoyés de Dieu du point de vue de leur identité purement spirituelle. Il y a une unité fondamentale dans leurs révélations et dans leurs messages: tous témoignent de l'«Un». Le Coran affirme à cet égard:

> Nous n'avons point envoyé avant toi d'apôtre à qui il n'ait été révélé qu'il n'y a point d'autre Dieu que moi.[4]

Et Yunus ne fait que le réitérer quand il dit que

> l'essentiel des quatre Livres Sacrés n'est rien d'autre, qu'il n'y a point de divinité en dehors de Dieu lui-même.

---

[3] Le Coran, XXXIII/72.
[4] Le Coran, XXI/25.

Ces Homme(s) Parfait(s) présentent deux particularités principales: la première, c'est de se poser en situation d'entière passivité face à l'Absolu et, la seconde, de recevoir la Science infuse, directement de Dieu, sans aucun intermédiaire créé.

Nous comprenons donc fort bien que, dans l'esprit de Yunus, l'homme n'est pas abandonné à son sort, soumis aux influences terrestres. Il a un chemin à parcourir. Il lui faut donc dépasser son moi, son propre égoïsme dans une dynamique qui lui permette de réaliser sa nature humaine au sens idéal du mot. Mais quelle voie l'homme doit-il suivre pour dépasser sa nature terrestre?

Il semble qu'à un premier niveau, l'homme doive prendre conscience de sa situation par rapport à l'ensemble des êtres de l'Univers, c'est-à-dire qu'il doit approfondir la connaissance de sa propre âme en découvrant la nature. Car celle-ci est un «miroir». En quelque sorte, l'intimité du rapport avec le Créateur commence par l'intimité de l'homme avec les autres créatures. En effet, aux yeux des soufis, l'homme est le prototype de l'Univers. Il y a un rapport microcosme/macrocosme entre l'homme et l'Univers, le premier étant le centre du second, car il est le point culminant vers lequel se polarise toute la création. L'homme doit donc se servir de sa position dans l'Univers pour tendre à l'unité de tous les êtres qui y existent. Il ne faut pas oublier, d'autre part, que les musulmans conçoivent l'Univers comme «le lieu d'ordre, de beauté, d'harmonie, de modèle, d'équilibre et de justice».

Mais il semble que dans la marche vers soi-même, l'Univers comme modèle d'équilibre et de justice ne suffit pas à l'homme. Il a également besoin d'un modèle humain ayant déjà parcouru le même chemin, d'un «autrui» qui lui servira de guide. C'est là qu'apparaît la nécessité du maître spirituel.

Dans le soufisme en général, ce maître – que Yunus connut en la personne de Taptuk Emre – est l'homme qui corrige les mauvais penchants de l'adepte, en lui purifiant le coeur, en lui dévoilant la lumière qui est au fond de lui. L'enseignement ne se fonde nullement sur les mots, ni sur les syllogismes qui ne susciteraient chez le disciple que des effets extérieurs ou rationnels. Il s'agit plutôt d'une initiation par la transmission d'un message s'adressant au plus intime de l'âme, et au moyen d'un accord spirituel. En réalité, le guide humain n'est autre qu'un substitut du guide intérieur, seul principe conduisant à l'Identité Suprême. Il doit donc savoir amener la rencontre harmonieuse entre le moi et le maître intérieur.

La marche, l'évolution vers soi-même s'effectue, étape par étape, en traversant des «stations spirituelles». Mais le but final n'est qu'en réalité le point de départ. En effet, la conscience religieuse de l'islam est fondée sur un événement primordial, qui est antérieur au temps de son histoire, dans ce monde de génération et de corruption. C'est le pacte préexistant entre l'homme et Dieu, si bien expliqué dans le verset coranique:

> Souvenez-vous que Dieu tira un jour des reins des fils d'Adam tous leurs descendants et leur fit rendre un témoignage contre eux. Il leur dit 'Ne suis-je pas votre Seigneur?'. Ils répondirent 'Oui, nous l'attestons'.[5]

Il y a là un dialogue avec Dieu, antérieur à la conscience de l'homme en tant que telle. Pourtant, ce dialogue se cache dans le secret intime de son coeur.

C'est d'ailleurs dans l'unique affirmation de ce «oui» que l'homme devient lui-même. Toute la démarche mystique musulmane consiste alors en un retour à cet état primordial qui se définit comme le secret intime, entièrement pénétré par Dieu. Là, toute acquisition possédée au nom de soi doit être éliminée pour parvenir à l'anéantissement, jusqu'au moment où l'homme ne trouve que la Présence Divine, qui est la qualification de son état primordial dans toute sa réalité ontologique. Il s'agit donc ici d'un effacement du moi devant la divinité, pour ne faire place qu'à une plénitude du Créateur. En même temps, l'homme se dépouille de sa personnalité pour ne se reconnaître qu'en Dieu. Les soufis appellent cet état «anéantissement de soi» (*al fanā'*). Cela ne signifie nullement un état de non-être car c'est dans une telle situation spirituelle que l'homme trouve la source de son être et aboutit à la permanence (*al Baqā'*), c'est-à-dire à ce qui, en lui, est absolu et nécessaire. Dans un tel état, les limites individuelles qui forment un voile entre l'homme et le secret intime dont il est porteur au tréfonds de son être sont abolies. D'où le sens du verset coranique

> Tout sur elle (la Terre) est évanescent; il ne subsistera que la face de ton Seigneur, essence de la Majesté et de la Générosité.[6]

C'est donc par rapport à ce dernier aspect qu'apparaît de façon certaine la doctrine de l'Unicité de l'existence dans la pensée de Yunus Emre. Il faut reconnaître que cette doctrine joue un rôle principal chez Yunus, comme chez tous les autres soufis vécus sur le territoire turc à partir du XIIIème siècle.

---

[5] Le Coran, VII/170.
[6] Le Coran, LV/26-27.

Certes, l'Unicité de Dieu est la doctrine fondamentale dans la pensée islamique. Mais dans cette affirmation de l'Unicité divine, il y a, semble-t-il, différents degrés. Il faut certainement en comprendre le sens vrai et profond, ce qui suppose une réalisation intérieure. C'est ce à quoi Yunus nous invite.

Comme les autres soufis, il observe à propos de l'Unicité divine, trois catégories. La première est celle du sens commun qui confirme l'Unicité dans son aspect extérieur et suit au pied de la lettre les commandements prescrits. La deuxième est celle des «gens de la science» et de la raison, qui se fonde essentiellement sur la démonstration: ce sont les gens de la certitude scientifique (ʿilm al-yaqūn), des savoirs extérieurs propres des théologiens et philosophes qui soumettent les Vérités Divines à des critères rationnels. Quant-à la troisième catégorie, c'est là, d'après Yunus, le véritable niveau de la foi (Imān), car la foi y est prise dans toute sa spiritualité. Ici, pour reprendre les termes de Roger Arnaldez, le fidèle s'élève

> à partir du Dieu qui parle dans la loi, jusqu'au Dieu qui parle dans le coeur.[7]

C'est à ce stade que la réalisation personnelle de l'Unicité prend le nom de Maʿrifa (gnose). Il s'agit là du lieu de la plus grande certitude.

A ce dernier niveau, l'ordre de la raison est entièrement dépassé et la validité extérieure des raisonnements démonstratifs laisse la place à l'Un Absolu. Il y a là une expérience inspirée qui est le propre de la connaissance mystique et qui n'est autre que la conscience d'un contact direct avec Dieu.

En guise de conclusion, nous pouvons affirmer que Yunus invite l'homme à s'éveiller à lui-même car, par ce réveil, il trouvera sa dignité d'être. Mais notre poète ne condamne pas l'homme à lui-même, car l'essence de ce dernier n'est que ce dépassement vers l'Unité absolue de toute chose. C'est par l'anéantissement de tout ce qui, dans l'homme, est relatif et contingent qu'il amène à un réveil à soi-même. Mais ce réveil ne peut avoir lieu que dans l'Essence de tous les Etres qui n'est, en réalité, que la Divine Vérité.

---

[7] Roger Arnaldez; article "La mystique musulmane", dans *La mystique et les mystiques*, p. 621, Paris.

Some Elements of the Mysticism of St. Francis
in the Thirteenth Century Context

Prof. Dr William Henn OFM Cap.

While it would be difficult if not impossible to summarize all of the writings about the prayer-life or the spirituality of Francis of Assisi, the number of studies devoted precisely to the «mysticism» of St. Francis is surprisingly small.[1] This may be in part a result of the fact that the word «mysticism» is not found in Francis' writings themselves nor in the various early biographies of the

---

[1] "Despite the spate of writings about St. Francis, so far comparatively little attention has been given to his mysticism." So writes Octavian Schmucki, OFM Cap., "The Mysticism of St. Francis in Light of His Writings," *Greyfriars Review* 3 (1989) 241-266, 241. This excellent article first appeared in German as "Zur Mystik des hl. Franziskus von Assisi im Lighte seiner 'Schriften'," in Kurt Ruh, ed., *Abendländische Mystik im Mittelalter* (Stuttgart, 1986) pp. 241-268 and begins with a critical review of eight previous works which deal with the mysticism of St. Francis: Daniel Howard Sinclair Nicholson, *The Mysticism of St. Francis* (London-Boston, 1923; Leo Bracaloni, "S. Francesco nella sua vita mistica," *Studi Francescani* 26 (1929) 423-476 and idem., "La spiritualità francescana ascetica e mistica," ibid. 37 (1940) 7-31; Maria Pia Borghese Freschi, *L'esperienza mistica di S. Francesco d'Assisi* (Palermo, 1930); Cuthbert Hess, "The Mysticism of St. Francis of Assisi: His Sacramental View of the Visible Wold," *Ecclesiastical Review* 87 (1932) 225-237; Kurt Ruh, "Zur Grundlegung einer Geschichte der franziskanischen Mystik," in idem. ed *Altdeutsch und altniederländische Mystik* (Darmstadt, 1964) pp. 240-274; Robert Cancik, "Grundzüge franziskanischer Leidensmystik," in idem., *Rausch - Ekstase - Mystik* (Düsseldorf, 1978), pp. 95-119; Anton Rotzetter, "Franz von Assisi, Lebensprogramm - Grunderfahrung," in A. Rotzetter et al., *Ein Anfang und was davon bleibt* (Zürich-Einsiedeln-Köln, 1981), pp. 17-163, 335-341; Isnard Wilhelm Frank, "Frömmigkeit und Gotteserfahrung des hl. Franziskus," in idem. *Franz von Assisi* (Düsseldorf, 1982) pp. 34-100. Schmucki then offers his own interpretation based primarily on the writings of St. Francis. Several points in the following paper will follow Schmucki rather closely.

saint.[2] Thus some would prefer to speak of Francis' «experience of God» rather than of his «mysticism.» Furthermore, as many authors have pointed out, the word mysticism itself is prone to a wide variety of definitions or descriptions, not all of which are mutually compatible.[3] This too may account in part for the scarcity of writings about Francis' mysticism. In this paper, I will consider Francis' «mysticism» simply as his immediate experience of and relationship with God as well as some of the characteristics of this relationship and the effects it has upon his dealings with other human beings and with the whole of creation.

The following comments will be divided into two sections. First, I will provide some indications about the spiritual climate of the early thirteenth century within Christianity and about life and writings of Francis of Assisi. In the second section I will outline some of the essential aspects of Francis' mysticism.

Part I: Times, Life and Writings of Francis of Assisi

Joseph Jungmann, in his short history of Christian prayer, notes that the turn of the eleventh and twelfth centuries marked a shift toward a new focus in Christian spirituality:

... a sense of the concrete suddenly reveals itself.[4]

---

[2] Schmucki, p. 246, writes: "Every reader is aware of the great difference between Francis's writings and the autobiographical revelations of other mystics. ... The vocabulary used by mystic writers of his time, such as *contemplatio, extasis, gustus, mysticus, raptus, speculatio, via purgativa/illuminativa/perfectiva*, is lacking in his writings.

[3] Harvey D. Egan SJ, *What Are They Saying about Mysticism?* (New York: Paulist, 1982) pp. 1, states: "To do full justice to the contemporary interest and research in the mystical traditions of the East and West, psychology, the occult, altered states of consciousness, psychedelic drug experiences, charismatic phenomena, etc., would perhaps require listing several hundred, often irreconcilable definitions of mysticism." On pages 2-3 he settles for the following description: "Although this book will present authors who define mysticism in a vast variety of ways, perhaps mysticism can be tentatively defined as the universal thrust of the human spirit for experiential union with the Absolute and the theory of that union." It is surprising that Egan speaks of «thrust» rather than of the attainment of union. G. Moioli, "Mistica Cristiana", in *Nuovo Dizionario di Spiritualità* (Roma: Paoline, 1979) p. 985, conveys more the sense of mysticism as realization, when he offers this heuristic description: mysticism is "... that moment or level or expression of religious experience in which a particular religious world comes to be lived as an experience of interiority and immediacy." A recent attempt to state what mysticism is, written in the context of western Christian mysticism during the middle ages is Alois M. Haas, "Was ist Mystik?," in *Abendländische Mystik im Mittelalter*, pp. 319-341.

[4] Joseph Jungmann, *Christian Prayer through the Centuries* (New York: Paulist, 1978), p. 96.

Christians became more interested in meditating upon the very empirical aspects of Jesus' life, particularly of his birth and his suffering and death. This focus harmonized with the two principal liturgical feasts of Christmas and Easter.[5] Contemplation of the life of Jesus carried with it the imperative to imitate his life.

This intention to imitate Jesus and the earliest Christian community gave rise to some of the «apostolic life» movements such as the Poor of Lyon, under the inspiration of Peter Waldo, or the Cathari, the pure.[6] Some of these movements stressed voluntary poverty to the point of adopting a rather Manichean condemnation of material goods and, in particular, a rejection of Church ownership of property; as such, they form a clear contrast with the notion of poverty to be found in the spirituality of St. Francis. As we shall see, his mysticism, while demanding a rather rigorous self-renunciation with regard to the use of material goods, seemed to delight in the visible world as an indication of God's goodness and as a motive to praise God.[7]

The beginning of the thirteenth century is not listed as one of the principal eras of Christian mysticism by Evelyn Underhill in the historical sketch with which she concludes her classic study of mysticism. Underhill indicates three great waves of mystical activity, reaching their highest points in the third, fourteenth and seventeenth centuries.[8] The prayer tradition to which Francis was heir was much less that of Pseudo-Dionysius, Bernard of Clairvaux and others who were to influence the great mystics of later centuries, than that of the simple meditative, litany-like prayer, common among the laity, in which Pater nosters were repeated over and again while one reflected on some aspects of the life of Jesus.[9]

---

[5] Jungmann, p. 112. For the rise of devotionalism that characterized this age, see Richard Kieckhefer, "Major Currents in Late Medieval Devotion," in Jill Raitt, ed. *Christian Spirituality: High Middle Ages and Reformation* (London, 1987), pp. 75-108. In the same collection of essays one finds the useful contribution by J.A. Wayne Hellmann, "The Spirituality of the Franciscans," pp. 31-50.

[6] On these movements, see George Tavard, "Apostolic Life and Church Reform," in *Christian Spirituality: High Middle Ages and Reformation*, pp. 1-11.

[7] The article by Cuthbert Hess, cited in note 1, has been a very influential proponent of the setting Francis' mysticism within the context of a positive view of nature. See also Edward A. Armstrong, *Saint Francis: Nature Mystic. The Derivation and Significance of the Nature Stories in the Franciscan Legend* (Berkeley-Los Angeles-London, 1973).

[8] Evelyn Underhill, *Mysticism* (New York, 1961), p. 454.

[9] On the popularity of such repetitive prayer, see Schmucki, p. 245 and Jungmann, pp. 103-109.

Francis of Assisi was born in 1182, the son of a wealthy Assisian cloth merchant, Pietro Bernadone, and his French born wife, Pia. His youth was spent acquiring a rudimentary education, working in his father's business, enjoying the finer possessions and revels which were available to him because of his father's wealth and dreaming of becoming a famous knight. In 1205, after a period of imprisonment at the hands of the Perugians following the battle of Collestrada and after a long illness, Francis begins to feel God's call to devote himself to more extensive periods of prayer.[10] Once in a dream he heard a voice ask:

Francis, whom is it better to serve, the master or the servant?,

a question which led him to think that his life was to be spent in service to God and not some human master. On another occasion, while praying in the dilapidated little church of San Damiano, he heard a voice from the painted crucifix which said:

Repair my House, which you see is in ruins.

He responded literally and rebuilt not only that chapel but also two other abandoned churches. Another important moment in his process of conversion was his meeting a leper along the road from Foligno to Assisi. Francis was naturally generous and known for his charity to the poor, but he was of a delicate, poetic nature and felt much revulsion at the sight and smell of lepers. Overcoming his natural feelings, he descended from his horse and kissed the leper, and what before had been bitter was changed into sweetness. He began to take care of lepers at a leprosarium not far from Assisi and the whole experience of overcoming himself so as to serve them was so significant that, when he wrote his *Testament* shortly before his death, he recalls it as the turning point in his life.

His behavior in no way pleased his father and led to their dramatic encounter before the bishop of Assisi in which Francis returned to his father what money he had as well as the clothing he was wearing. Henceforth he would live simply as a child of God, according to the prayer of Jesus, the "Our Father." Shortly thereafter, he and several other young men who were impressed by his courageous attempt to devote himself to God were inspired to literally follow the gospel texts which speak about selling all that one has and following Jesus (Mk 10,13-31) and about taking nothing for the journey but going throughout the world to proclaim the kingdom of God (Mt 10,7-42). As it turned out, those

---

[10] A handy chronology for the life of St. Francis can be found in Marion A. Habig, ed. *St. Francis of Assisi. Writings and Early Biographies* (Chicago, c. 1973), pp. xi-xiv.

texts set the pattern for Francis' life for the next twenty years until his death in 1226. His life alternated between travels to preach and speak about Jesus, on the one hand, and long sojourns of prayer in isolated hermitages, on the other. The travels were mainly in Italy but included several attempts to reach territories where Muslims were predominant. According to a number of his biographers he was successful once and met the Sultan Malik al Kamil at Damietta in 1219.[11] His sojourns in prayer were spent in small hermitages tucked away in mountain forests – places like Fonte Colombo, Greccio or Poggio Bustone in the Rieti valley or high on the mountain La Verna.

Even during his lifetime several thousand men left their former occupations to live like Francis, as well as a group of women under the leadership of St. Clare who adopted the life of poverty as cloistered nuns and many lay people who sought to incorporate the values which Francis stressed in his life and preaching within the context of their family lives. To these many followers he provided guidelines for a way of life, always seeking the approval, guidance and protection of the leaders of the Catholic Church.

His last two years were marked by much physical suffering, particularly by a painful eye disease which ultimately left him blind. He died, lying naked on the ground and listening to the reading of the gospel account of Jesus' passion and death.

Finally, a word is in order about the written sources which can serve as the basis for commenting on the mysticism of Francis of Assisi. There are two primary sources about his life which come down to us from the thirteenth century: his own writings and about ten different biographies. His own writings enjoy a priority over the biographies not only because they are directly from Francis but, in addition, because the biographies were written by representatives

---

[11] See Francis De Beer, "St. Francis and Islam, "*Concilium* 149 (1981) 11-20, for an overview of the various accounts of Francis' encounter with the Sultan and for suggestions about the way in which this encounter altered Francis' vision of things. Some have suggested that the deep impression which the call to prayer by the muezzin (*muᶜadhdhin*) gave each day inspired the following sentence in Francis' *Letter to the Rulers of the Peoples*: "And you should manifest such honor to the Lord among the people entrusted to you that every evening an announcement be made by a town crier or some other signal that praise and thanks may be given by all people to the all-powerful Lord God." This text is the translation found in Regis J. Armstrong and Ignatius C. Brady, *Francis and Clare. The complete Works* (New York-Ramsey-Toronto, 1982), p. 78. This translation is based on the definitive Latin (Italian for the *Canticle of the Creatures*) text edited by Kajetan Esser, *Opuscula Sancti Patris Francisci Assisiensis* (Grottaferrata, 1976). Further citations of Francis' writings in English will be taken from the Armstrong translation.

of groups who followed the poverty of Francis in varying degrees of strictness. In part, each of the various biographies was an attempt to justify its author's own interpretation of Francis and of how his followers should live.[12] That said, however, it must be added immediately that the biographies are more descriptive of the prayer life of St. Francis. They often put together a whole sequence of stories from his life for the purpose of describing the way Francis prayed.[13] In contrast, Francis' own writings are much more reticent to talk about his experience of God in prayer. Indeed, in one of them, he advises his followers never to disclose to others the gifts that God gives to them in prayer.[14] Nevertheless, in his writings – which all together add up to a rather small book and which fall into three categories: rules and admonitions for his followers, letters and prayers – Francis cannot hide his intense experience of and love for God. Thus while the writings do not intend to describe his mystical experience, they do offer the surest and most accurate port of access to his mysticism.[15]

Part II: Aspects of the Mysticism of Francis of Assisi

The *radical re-ordering* of his emotions and natural tendencies must be noted chronologically as the point of departure for Francis' mystical experience.[16] Yves Congar offers an illuminating interpretation of this radical self-

---

[12] A useful essay which illustrates the way in which various early sources reflect the biases of their authors is Malcolm Lambert, "The Problem of St. Francis," in his *Franciscan Poverty* (London, 1961) 1-30. A rather extensive bibliography including works up to the year 1969 which address the dating and historical value of the various writings and early biographies can be found in Habig, pp. 1681-1699. For more recent studies one can consult the Franciscan bibliographies published regularly by the *Collectanea Francescana*.

[13] For example, the *Second Life of St. Francis* by Thomas of Celano, paragraphs 94-101 (in Habig, pp. 439-446) or St. Bonaventure's *Major Life of St. Francis*, Chapter Ten (in Habig, pp. 705-711).

[14] *Admonition* XXI and, especially, XXVIII: "Blessed is that servant who stores up *in heaven* (Mt. 6:20) the good things which the Lord has revealed to him and does not desire to reveal them to others in the hope of profiting thereby, for the Most High Himself will manifest His deeds to whomever He wishes. Blessed is the servant who keeps the secrets of the Lord in his heart (cf. Lk 2:19, 51)." In Armstrong, pp. 34 and 36.

[15] This is one of the main points of Schmucki in criticizing earlier works on the mysticism of St. Francis, that is, that they draw almost exclusively on the biographies and do not take advantage of the insights which can be gleaned from the saint's words themselves. The current tendency in Franciscan scholarship gives priority to Francis' own writings as historical sources for reconstructing whatever particular aspect of his life one may be interested in.

[16] Schmucki, p. 247.

renunciation in his short essay about Francis entitled "Pilgrim of the Absolute."[17] Congar explains that the world of thirteenth century Italy was highly structured according to the various civil and ecclesiastical orders. Francis' desire to devote himself to God took symbolic form in two actions in which he radically broke out of the given order of things: the renunciation of his patrimony as the son of Pietro Bernadone and the renunciation of his natural interior inclinations with the kissing of the leper. The first renunciation placed Francis outside of the structures which governed society in his time; the second freed him from his own likes and dislikes. These symbolic actions of self-renunciation were moments of great liberation which allowed Francis to begin to live for God alone, and not on the basis of what others might expect of him or on the basis of his own personal preference.

This radical re-ordering of the bases of his activity was not a once and for all accomplishment, but rather needed to be reinforced at regular intervals throughout his lifetime by periods of fasting and other forms of self renunciation, periods which he also mandated for his followers in his Rule.[18] He writes:

> For the spirit of the flesh desires and is most eager to have words, but [cares] little to carry them out. And it does not seek a religion and holiness in the interior spirit, but it wishes and desires to have a religion and holiness outwardly apparent to people. ... But the Spirit of the Lord wishes the flesh to be mortified and despised, worthless and rejected.[19]

This theme of mortifying ones's lower nature is predominant in his letter written to all the faithful, which is basically structured upon a comparison between those who do penance and those who do not.[20] In another text, the tenth of his *Admonitions*, Francis writes:

> ... each one has the [real] enemy in his power; that is, the body through which he sins. Therefore *blesses is that servant* (Mt 24:46) who, having such an enemy in his power, will always hold him captive and wisely

---

[17] Yves Congar, *Pellegrino dell'Assoluto. L'Assoluto del Vangelo nella Cristianità* (Milano, 1962). A more satisfying version because it includes the footnotes which were provided with the original essay is entitled: "San Francesco d'Assisi o l'assoluto del vangelo nella cristianità," in idem., *Le vie del Dio vivo* (Brescia, 1965), pp. 219-235.

[18] So *The Earlier Rule*, Chapter 3, in Armstrong, p. 112; and *The Later Rule*, Chapter 3, in Armstrong, p. 139.

[19] *The Earlier Rule*, Chapter 17, in Armstrong, p. 123.

[20] See the two versions of the *Letter to the Faithful* in Armstrong, pp. 62-73.

guard himself against him, because as long as he does this, no other enemy, seen or unseen, will be able to harm him.[21]

Such renunciation, suggests Congar, not only freed Francis to devote himself radically to the love and service of God but also explains Francis' choice to live as a poor man. Poverty was not, first and foremost, an act of imitating Jesus or the apostles but rather the condition for concentrating more purely and wholeheartedly on the fundamental relationship with God. In the Rule Francis writes:

> This is that summit of highest poverty which has established you, my most beloved brothers, as heirs and kings of the kingdom of heaven; it has made you poor in the things [of this world] but exalted you in virtue (cf. Ja 2:5).[22]

This freedom leads to a second fundamental aspect of Francis' mysticism – *passivity*. In Francis' *Testament*, a document of special meaningfulness because it was written close to the time of the saint's death with the intention of recounting the essential aspects of his way of life, God is very often the active subject of the narrative. He writes:

> God inspired me, Brother Francis, to embark upon a life of penance...
> ... God led me into the company of lepers and I had pity on them. God inspired me with faith in churches ... and ... with faith in priests.... When God gave me some friars, there was no one to tell me what I should do; but the Most High himself made it clear to me that I must live the life of the Gospel. God revealed a form of greeting to me, telling me that we should say, 'God give you peace.' ... God inspired me to write the Rule and these words plainly and simply, and so you too must understand them plainly and simply, and live by them, doing good to the last.

Schmucki comments on this recurrent theme of the *Testament* in which God appears as the agent and Francis is merely the instrument or the one being fashioned by the activity of God:

> In all the changing circumstances of his life he experiences God as his true guide. He senses God operating immanently and deeply in all his

---

[21] Armstrong, pp. 30-31. In the charming story about «perfect joy,» Francis tells brother Leo that among all the graces which God bestows upon his friends, the best is "that of conquering oneself and willingly enduring sufferings, insults, humiliations, and hardships for the love of Christ." See *The Little Flowers*, number 8, in Habig, pp. 1318-1320.

[22] *The Later Rule*, Chapter 6, Armstrong, p. 141.

human activities, without thereby depriving him of his freedom of action or personal responsibility.[23]

Such passivity is illustrated in events such as the time when he opened the scriptures three times to learn God's will for himself and his first companions.[24] Another example is a legend from *The Little Flowers* which tells of a journey in which Francis and Brother Masseo came to a crossroads and, wanting to follow in the direction which God wished, Francis asked Masseo to close his eyes, twirl around and suddenly stop. They took the road so indicated, judging it to be the way which God wanted them to travel.[25] Such an attitude in the small details of daily life appears also in more weighty matters such as the rule of life which Francis wrote for his followers. It begins and ends with a brief summary stating that the whole life of the friars minor is to observe the gospel.[26]

The effort always to carry out the will of God reflects Francis' effort to live continually in the presence of God, to be always pliant and receptive to the ways in which God wished him to act at any particular moment. This theme comes to expression whenever Francis speaks about work. He writes:

> Those brothers to whom the Lord has given the grace of working should do their work faithfully and devotedly so that, avoiding idleness, the enemy of the soul, they do not extinguish the Spirit of holy prayer and devotion to which all other things of our earthly existence must contribute.[27]

This applies also to learning.

> And those who are illiterate should not be eager to learn. Instead let them pursue what they must desire above all things: to have the Spirit of the Lord and His holy manner of working, to pray always to Him with a pure heart....[28]

---

[23] Schmucki, p. 248. A lovely expression of this intention to perform the will of God is the prayer from early in Francis' conversion, which Armstrong, p. 103, translates thus: "Most high, glorious God, enlighten the darkness of my heart and give me, Lord, a correct faith, a certain hope, a perfect charity, sense and knowledge, so that I may carry out Your holy and true command."

[24] So Thomas of Celano's *Second Life*, 15 (Habig, pp. 374-375); Bonaventure's *Major Life*, Chapter III, 3 (Habig, pp. 647-648); *Legend of the Three Companions*, 28-29 (Habig, pp. 917-918) and *The Little Flowers*, 2 (Habig, pp. 1302-1305).

[25] *The Little Flowers*, 11, in Habig p. 1323.

[26] For the precise texts, see Armstrong, pp. 137 and 145.

[27] *The Later Rule*, Chapter 5, in Armstrong, p. 140.

[28] *The Later Rule*, Chapter 10, in Armstrong, p. 144.

Francis' own unceasing prayer was the context for his *experience of God*, the very heart of his mysticism. Above all else he experienced God as good. In three of his writings Francis breaks into a short hymn of praise to the goodness of God:

> Therefore let us desire nothing else, let us wish for nothing else, let nothing else please us and cause us delight except our Creator and Redeemer and Savior, the one true God, who is the Fullness of Good, all good, every good, the true and supreme good, who alone is Good, merciful and gentle, delectable and sweet, who alone is holy, just and true, holy and right, who alone is kind, innocent, pure, from whom and through whom and in whom is all pardon, all grace, all glory of all the penitent and the just, of all the blessed who rejoice together in heaven.[29]

Schmucki's comment on this text brings out nicely the elements of mysticism which can be located within it. He writes:

> The recurrence of emotionally charged verbs and adjectives – to desire, to will, to please, to enjoy; God the good, sweet, and so forth – is an awareness of God's goodness. Like other mystics, Francis was incapable of adequately expressing his innermost experiences. He therefore praises the divine goodness and holiness in a torrent of synonyms and repeats the same adjectives even in the one sentence. He plays all kinds of variations on the theme of divine goodness. God is the only good, since this attribute properly belongs to Him alone. He is eternally as well as truly good, because He contains every kind of created good in the highest degree. He is the source from which all other good things flow and to which they are drawn. This God who stoops down to man in boundless love is not the object of theological speculation but of loving relish. The frequent use of the same phrases and concepts in Francis' writings calls to mind a form of mystical prayer like the so-called Jesus Prayer, or prayer of the heart, which was in use from early Christian times. We must not, however, overlook the fact that in contrast to the Jesus Prayer, that of Francis was theocentric.[30]

This understanding of the goodness of God leads Francis to attribute all goodness which he sees in the world to the work of God. Thus in his Eighth Admonition he considers envy of the good which someone else does as a form of blasphemy, insofar as the ultimate source of the good, even of the actions, of others is always

---

[29] *The Earlier Rule*, Chapter 23, in Armstrong, p. 133; see also the *Parchment Given to Brother Leo*, in Armstrong, p. 100, and *The Praises to Be Said at All the Hours*, in Armstrong, p. 102.

[30] Schmucki, pp. 250-251.

God himself.[31] The goodness and benevolence of God lead Francis to follow the New Testament in characterizing God as love.[32]

Perhaps one of the most forceful expressions of Francis' experience of God can be found in his *Praises of God*, a prayer which he wrote shortly after what his biographers indicate as one of his most intense experiences of God, that during the weeks of August and September of 1224 on the mountain of La Verna.[33] This prayer takes the form of a litany in which all but three of lines begin with the Latin word «Tu» – «You». Scholars have divided the hymn into three unequal stanzas. The first stanza praises God for working great marvels and then applies various adjectives to him:

> You are holy; You are strong; You are great; You are the most high; You are omnipotent,

ending with Francis' typical reference to God's goodness:

> You are the good, all good, the highest good.

The second and longer stanza addressed Gob by using substantives, nouns which stand for qualities or values which are prized by human beings:

> You are love; You are wisdom; You are patience, beauty, meekness, security, tranquility, joy, happiness,

and so forth. Moreover, as if in the enthusiasm of a mystic encounter with God, the prayer seems to build up to a crescendo, an aspect brought out by the repetition with ever increasing frequency of the adjective «noster» – «our».

> You are our guardian and defender; You are strength; You are refuge; You are our hope, You are our faith, You are our charity; You are all our sweetness; You are our eternal life.

---

[31] *Admonitions*, VIII, in Armstrong, p. 30; on the same page see also admonition VII, on God as source of all good.

[32] He quotes 1 Jn 4,16 to this effect in the *Letter to the Faithful* (Armstrong, pp. 65 and 73), and in *The Later Rule*, Chapter 22 (Armstrong, p. 128).

[33] Accounts about the experience of St. Francis on La Verna can be found in Thomas of Celano's *First Life of St. Francis*, 94-96 (in Habig, pp. 308-311); Bonaventure's *Major Life*, Chapter XIII (Habig, pp. 729-736); Bonaventure's *Minor Life*, Chapter VI (Habig, pp. 821-826); and *The Little Flowers*, Part II (Habig, pp. 1429-1474). For an excellent treatment of the *Praises of God*, see Leonhard Lehmann, "Das Schriftstück für Bruder Leo," in idem. *Tiefe und Weite. Der universale Grundzug in den Gebet des Franziskus von Assisi* (Werl/Westfalen, 1984) 247-277.

A final and very brief third stanza summarizes the whole prayer:

Great and wonderful Lord God, almighty and merciful savior.

Thus this prayer constitutes a litany of names for God, names which might be understood as the stammering praise of one caught up in a mystical ecstasy.[34] The first stanza focuses on God in Himself, as strong and good; the second enumerates some of the many ways in which God's goodness shows itself to us human beings; and the third short stanza ties these two notions together in a final acclamation – the great and wonderful Lord is also our merciful savior. Thus the prayer ends with God's great mercy.

Ending with the note of mercy is particularly fitting when one realizes that these *Praises of God* were written as a gift for a friend who was suffering from some spiritual discouragement and who felt he would be consoled if he had some words written by Francis.[35] Francis wrote the prayer on one side of a parchment and on the other wrote a blessing for this friend, Brother Leo. The blessing is simply a quotation of the one given in Numbers 6,24-26 (which begins "May the Lord bless you and keep you"), with the addition of the final words

May the Lord bless you, Brother Leo.[36]

What is noteworthy here is the fact that, in a way similar to the *Praises of God*, the word «you» is also very prominent in the *Blessing for Brother Leo*. But here in the blessing the «you» is not God but rather Francis' troubled friend. The coincidence of these two «you's» on the two sides of one piece of parchment – in one case, the divine You, whom Francis praises and whose mercy toward humankind he admires, and in the other case, the human you, who is his troubled brother, Leo – this coincidence shows the *close relation between loving God and loving one's fellow man* in the mystical experience of St. Francis. In loving and contemplating God, Francis recognized God's tremendous mercy and love for all people and this, in turn, inspired Francis to love all others as his brothers and sisters.

---

[34] See Lehmann, p. 275.

[35] So Celano's *Second Life*, 49, in Habig, p. 406; and Bonaventure's *Major Life*, Chapter XI, 9, in Habig, p. 717. See also Lehmann, pp. 276-277 for an inspiring summary about this Parchment given to Brother Leo.

[36] For the complete text, see Armstrong, pp. 99-100.

Francis' mystical experience of God not only informed the way in which he perceived his fellow human beings but also fashioned his *understanding of nature*. In fact the popular image of his piety can leave one with the impression that his mysticism was focused upon nature. With regard to the various publications about the saint, Schmucki notes:

> Almost all writers recognize Francis' relationship with nature as something truly extraordinary.[37]

His appreciation of nature would have been formed, first of all, by his knowledge of the psalms, which comprised part of his education in the parish school of San Giorgio when he was growing up and which he prayed regularly throughout his adult life as part of the official prayer of the Church.[38] Now many of these psalms, such as 8, 19, 29, 104 and 148, explicitly foster a religious view of nature as God's creation. A further point to keep in mind with regard to Francis' attitude toward nature is the fact that much of his life was spent out of doors. His promise of poverty resulted in the situation that the hermitages and places where he and his friars lived were generally exposed to the outdoors and, when Francis was not living in such places he was travelling through the countryside as an itinerant preacher and worker. His overall devotion to God and to the praise of God would naturally have embraced what God had accomplished in the creation within which he lived and moved and to the beauty of which he was so sensitive.

In the *Canticle of the Creatures*, also called the *Canticle of Brother Sun*, Francis' praise of God because of creation received its consummate expression. It was written in the spring of 1225, during a period in which Francis was suffering great pain because of his eye disease, so much so that he remained within a darkened room during the day on account of the fact the light gave his eyes great discomfort. In his discouragement one night he prayed to God, who

---

[37] Schmucki, p. 258. Some indications from the early sources about Francis' love for creation and the way in which it moved him to love the Creator are: Bonaventure, *Major Life*, Chapter IX,1 (Habig, p. 698) and the *Mirror of Perfection*, Chapter XI (Habig, pp. 1252-1261).

[38] Francis prayed the Divine Office and legislated in the Rules that it be prayed by his friars (cf. Armstrong, pp. 111-112, 139). He confesses to not having prayed the office with enough fidelity and devotion in *A Letter to the Entire Order* (cf. Armstrong, p. 59). His intimate knowledge of the psalms can be seen in the way in which he strings together phrases and sentences drawn from them to form *The Office of the Passion* (cf. Armstrong, pp. 80-98). In his *Testament*, he considers the recitation of the Liturgy of the Hours according the norms of the Roman church so important that those friars who either do not pray the office or who alter it are treated as non-Catholics (cf. Armstrong, pp. 155-156).

consoled him with the confidence that he would one day enter into God's kingdom. The next morning he felt obliged to thank God, saying:

> ... for His glory, for my consolation, and the edification of my neighbor, I wish to compose a new 'Praises of the Lord' for His creatures. These creatures minister to our needs every day; without them we could not live; and through them the human race greatly offends the Creator. Every day we fail to appreciate so great a blessing by not praising as we should the Creator and dispenser of all these gifts.[39]

And after a few moments of thought he began the words of the Canticle:

> Most High, Almighty and Good Lord...

In this hymn, Francis praises God first for the three heavenly bodies which adorn the skies – the sun, the moon and the stars – and procedes to praise God for the four elements – air, water, fire and earth. In each stanza he calls these fellow creatures brother or sister, points out some of their good qualities (for example, that water is useful and refreshing or that the earth provides food and flowers), and praises God because of this goodness. He later added stanzas which honored God for those human beings who grant pardon and make peace and, as he was approaching his own death, in praise of God for Sister Death, who opens the door to eternal life. Francis experience of God transformed the way he saw the world.

Conclusion

When Gilbert Kieth Chesterton characterized the appearance of Saint Francis in the world of the thirteenth century, he said that it was as if the old world of Greek and Roman mythology had finally been purified. No longer was nature confused with God. He writes:

> The flowers and stars have recovered their first innocence. Fire and water are felt to be worthy to be the brother and sister of a saint. The purge of paganism is complete at last. For water itself has been washed. Fire itself has been purified as by fire. Water is no longer that water into which slaves were flung to feed the fishes. Fire is no longer that fire through which children were passed to Moloch. ... Man has stripped from his soul the last rag of nature-worship, and can return to nature.[40]

---

[39] For the story of the writing of the Canticle of the Creatures and for the quotation given in the text, see *The Legend of Perugia*, 43-44, in Habig, pp. 1020-1025. For an excellent scholarly interpretation of the Canticle, see Leonhard Lehmann, "Der Sonnengesang," in *Tiefe und Weite*, pp. 279-324.

[40] Gilbert Keith Chesterton, *St. Francis of Assisi* (Garden City, 1962 [c. 1928]) 36.

Francis' mysticism was an experience of God as the one to whom he owed his complete obedience and love. He broke with the social system of his time and lived in poverty, so as to be free to carry out whatever the spirit of God inspired him to do. His love for God led to a love for his fellow human beings and for all of creation. In a way then, his mysticism was a fresh appearance – like the dawning of a new day – of that proper relationship between a human being and God and the world. As Chesterton puts it:

> While it was yet twilight a figure appeared silently and suddenly on a little hill above the city, dark against the fading darkness. For it was the end of a long and stern night, a night of vigil, not unvisited by stars. He stood with his hands lifted, as in so many statues and pictures, and about him was a burst of birds singing; and behind him was the break of day.[41]

---

[41] Chesterton, pp. 36-37.

Art and Architecture of Anatolia
In the Age of Yunus Emre

Prof. Dr Oluş Arık

It is an honour and a great pleasure for me to present a paper to this distinguished group of scholars at this seminar, held in memory of Yunus Emre, who taught the dignity of the human soul and the value of love and tolerance.

I realize that it is impossible for me to talk on all aspects of the art and architecture of Yunus's time, although it spans merely «a minute» in the long course of history. I shall therefore confine myself to some impressions and observations related to them, which I hope, will give you a general idea about the physical surrounding of Yunus Emre.

Yunus Emre has lived in an age of Turkey, when the Seljuk state came to an end after a prosperous period and an interregnum, the so-called *Beylik Period* (the period of the Turkoman Principalities) emerged.

The culture of Turkey in that age was a complex blending of three major cultures:
– Turco-Asian culture,
– Islamic culture,
and the *heritage* of the
– Pre-Turkic cultures.

Turco-Asian Culture was brought by the Seljuks who laid the foundations of the present day Turkey, after they won a victory over Byzantine armies at Malazgirt in 1071.

In this new home land, Roman cities and fortified Byzantine towns existed in considerable numbers. Though many of them were in a ruinous state, there was not much need for the Seljuks to found new towns.

After consolidating their power, the Seljuks established order; revitalized the economy; restored and enlarged the towns and recreated the proper milieu for the commercial and cultural activities.

A. Gabriel's rendering of **Kayseri** in Cappadocia (the second capital city of Seljuks), and the general view of today's **Amasya** (a secondary center of the Seljuk and Principalities periods) may help us to imagine the basic character of medieval Turkish towns.

Having assimilated the local influences, Seljuks developed an original architecture of their own, with a distinctive form, spatial composition and decoration.

Diyarıbekr (with the antique name: Amida) is a roughly circular shaped city of Seljuk era in southeastern Turkey and the center of the local Turkish dynasty, the *Artukids*. Its walls are decorated with original Turkish symbolic reliefs, such as winged lions, sphinx and eagles with monumental inscriptions.

We have not sufficient information on commercial buildings of the Seljuks serving as hotels, markets and the workshops in the cities. On the other hand, the Seljuks achieved a huge project to encourage the merchants to prefer the Anatolian routes:
- They located caravanserais (with the original name of *han*) on the highways with a distance from each other of about a day's journey.
- They restored the old bridges and roads, built new ones, lowered custom dues, safeguarded the security of caravans by armed escorts, and developed a simple insurance system: reimbursing the traders for their loss from the state treasury, if they would be robbed within the Seljuk territory.

Seljuk *hans* offered almost all the comforts of that age, and they were free of charge. They generally have two sections: a covered hall and a monumental forecourt. The covered hall section is mostly constructed in a form which resembles the Christian basilicas. There are also a few hans which consist of only the covered hall section.

Vaulted recesses called *îwân*, open on one side, were an international feature in Central Asiatic buildings since ancient times. Yet, to combine four îwâns in a cross-axial scheme with a central court, and use it as the standard type in common and official buildings, from caravanserais to great mosques, is one of the main Turkish contributions to the Islamic architecture.

One could expected that the first mosques in Turkey would be of this «Four-Îwân-Type» as they were in Iran, the main land of the Great Seljuk Empire. However, it is interesting to note that amongst the Seljuks mosques in Turkey, around a hundred in number, only the **Great Mosque at Malatya** can be regarded as the continuation of this type. And it was built at a fairly later date: 1224. And yet, this mosque is a deviation from the standard four-îwân-type, with its single îwân.

Seljuk mosques remaining in this new home-land, display a variety of planning and spatial experiments. The earliest ones are related rather to the «Early Islamic Mosque Types» of neighbouring Mesopotamia and Syria with their transversally oriented rectangular prayer halls.

The **Great Mosque at Diyarıbekr** (Amida) has a high central nave flanked by lateral aisles that run at right angles to it – apparently a simplified application of the plan scheme of Umayyad Great Mosque at Damascus.

Alaaddin Cami (mosque) in Konya was probably the Great Mosque of the capital. It has a prayer hall with two parts: the eastern part has a multi columnar plan; the west wing possesses a monumental *mihrab*-section with a big dome. The interesting facade composition of its monumental forecourt reflects Syrian influences with geometric interlace work of grey and white marble. The twin columns of the gallery, crowning this facade, must have been brought from Byzantine ruins of the region.

In the **Great Mosque of Mayyâfârıqîn** (Silvan) from 1156, we observe an amalgamation of this early Umayyad space organization type, with inner Asian domed cubic construction type, in an attempt to create a mature spatial composition with a central dome.

Many of the thirteenth century Seljuk mosques in Turkey, are of the so-called «Basilica-Type», with a longitudinally oriented prayer hall, a central nave and symmetrical aisles, running on both sides parallel to it.

Mengücek Prince Behram Şah, a vassal of Seljuks, has the **Great Mosque** built **in Divriği**, and his wife Princess Turan Melik founded the **hospital** adjacent to it in 1228. The mosque is an elaborate example of basilica-type mosques and one of the most interestingly decorated buildings in Seljuk Anatolia. Some art historians characterized the **north portal** of this mosque as «baroque» due to its decorations, having gigantic floral reliefs. The **west portal**, on the other hand, is called the «textile door of Divriği», because its stone carvings remind us of *Kilim* and carpet patterns in low relief technique.

The magnificent **portal of the hospital** section with its ribbed structure having clustered columns and with its monumental pointed arch, resembling the Gothic style, is called among the art historians as the «Gothic door of Divriği». On the pedestals of this portal are a couple of busts. Each bears a Seljuk crown with long hair below, and wings; all in a style which resembles the famous angel reliefs of Konya Citadel's portal. Local people believe that these figures depict the generous wife and husband who founded this complex.

In a group of mosques there is a large, monumental mihrab-dome surrounded by bays in different shapes that the other units of prayer hall. A second dome crowns the bay almost at the center of the hall. Originally, these second domes with a lantern at the top served as a light well. The mosque section of the **Huand Hatun complex** in Kayseri founded by the wife of Sultan Alaaddin Keykubad I, is an excellent example of this group. This complex is the largest one of the Seljuk era, at the same time. It is completed between the years 1237-1260. The complex comprises a mosque, a *medrese*, a mausoleum and a *hamam* (a Turkish bath).

Another interesting complex of Anatolian Seljuk period is the famous **Mevlânâ - Dergâh** at Konya. It was the central convent of the Mevlevî order. The centrally domed hall in this complex is *semâhâne*, where musical and symbolic ritual dance ceremonies were performed. Dervish cells are aligned along the courtyard. There are also small mosque chamber, workshop and kitchen facilities in this complex. Some of these structures were added at different times between the thirteenth and fifteenth centuries, under the Seljuk, Karaman and Ottoman rules.

A special group of Anatolian Seljuk mosques is constructed with rubble walls and at the interior, many rows of wooden posts support the wooden upper structure. To anticipate from their external appearance the wealth and warmth of the interior is almost impossible. **Eşrefoğlu Mosque** in Beyşehir and **Mahmud Bey Mosque** in Kasabaköy near Kastamonu are brilliantly representing this style. The capitals of their wooden posts are either beautifully carved or built of small pieces intricately nailed together and decorated with highly stylized floral paintings in red, black, gold, yellow, blue and green. The same delicately composed decoration covers the boards and beams of the ceiling. In **Sivrihisar Great Mosque** and **Ankara Aslanhane Mosque,** on the tops of the wooden posts and underneath, antique marble capitals are reused as capitals or as post-bases.

There are many relations in construction and decoration between these Anatolian ones and the Central Asian mosques with wooden posts and ceilings which are known to exist since eleventh century.

82

The mosques with a single domed cubic prayer hall present the most continuously used architectural type in Turkey. They are essentially small neighbourhood mosques from the Seljuk period, some having a vestibule or a portico at the entrance facade as we observe in **Sırçalı Mescid** at Konya.

In the early Islamic period, in other words, till the eleventh century, the mosque often functioned as the town-hall and educational institution as well as a place of worship. Starting with the eleventh century when the Turks assumed a leading role in the Islamic world, new institutions of higher learning, the *medrese*, came into being and they gained at the same time a certain type of building peculiar to medrese. Like the mosques of Great Seljuk Empire, this also is a building organized around a central court with four monumental îwâns, each situated at the middle of the four sides of the rectangular plan; between the îwâns there are the rows of cells. Medrese was the institution of *waqf* (pious endowment). The *waqfiye* (foundation's charter) specified the salaries of the lecturers, professors, assistants and other employees of the institution. In a medrese the education was free of charge and the students received a stipend paid by the waqf.

Medrese building in Anatolia displays interesting decorative and structural variations as do the mosques. Most of the Anatolian medreses have two îwâns, one in the entrance and the other opposite it, leading to the central court. **Twin-Minaret Medrese** of Erzurum has two stories; but the medreses are mostly single storied.

A new building type peculiar to Anatolian Seljuks is the «covered medrese». **İnce Minareli and Karatay Medreses**, both in Konya, are two masterpieces of this type. Their structure scheme with rooms and îwâns surrounding a central space is the same; only the central space here, is a large, covered salon, the upper structure of which is usually a dome. But in some examples, vaults borne on columns and arches cover this central volume.

It is interesting to note that Seljuks did not completely adapt the structural form and plan of the centrally domed basilicas in the architecture of mosques whereas they applied this style exactly in the covered courts of some medreses and *şifahanes* (hospitals).

The higher education district of Sıvas, in eastern central Turkey, only partly remained to us. The hospital of Seljuk Sultan İzzeddin Keykâvus from 1211-1229, the famous Gök Medrese built by Seljuk vizier Sahib Ata in 1272, Çifte Minareli Medrese and Buruciye Medrese, both built by Mongol notables, again in 1272, may give us an inspiration to imagine the medieval atmosphere of such sites in a Seljuk town.

The exterior of Seljuk buildings are rather simple. Basically, the decorations concentrate on the portal. Projecting from the facade, the portal is generally designed as a monument in itself like an arch of triumph.

The **portal of İnce Minareli medrese** in Konya is a unique masterpiece of Seljuk period. Its long, narrow, rectangular prism shaped mass had on the front, high relief compositions, which give the impression of abstract sculptures. The portal niche resembles the decorative curtains of a royal tent-entrance and appears as if textile work has petrified...

An interesting innovation in Anatolian Seljuk architecture is the combination of twin-minarets and portal. The **portal of Sahib Ata Mosque** built in Konya in 1258, was the first attempt for this composition, but the part above the pedestal of one of the minarets has not come down to this date.

It seems to have been a fashion to build domed, cubic mausolea in Islamic Central Asia, the one belonging to İsma'il the Samanid in Bukhara from 910, being the earliest. This type of mausoleum expanded towards Asia Minor during the eleventh and twelfth centuries.

From the beginning of eleventh century on, a new type of funerary monument became fashion: tomb-towers. A high body in cylindrical or prismatic form is terminated by a conical or pyramidical cap. This type also expanded towards Asia Minor.

Seljuk *türbes* (mausolea) in Anatolia are essentially two storied structures: the partially buried crypt is entered through a separate and mostly concealed door, which is a few steps below the ground level. Here, we have the actual graves with mummified body. Above the crypt, reached by a double or one sided staircase, is the body of the building which contains the *masjid* chamber with a mihrab and ornate, symbolic sarcophagus, commemorating the personage for whom the mausoleum was built.

Mama Hatun Mausoleum in Tercan, near Erzurum in east Turkey, from the beginning of the 13th century, is another unique funerary monument of the Seljuk era. A wide circular wall surrounds a circular precinct and at the center rises the tomb-tower itself. Each one of the eight faces of the türbe (mausoleum) is in semi-cylindrical form. The conical cap is likewise fluted. The interior of the türbe also has the undulating structural form. On the inside of the circular wall which encloses the actual türbe, are eleven deep niches in the form of pointed arches, that were designed to house some further graves.

The upper chamber of the **Döner Kümbet** (revolving tomb tower) in Kayseri, Cappadocia, from the last quarter of the 13th century, is a cylindrical structure whereas its outer form is a dodecagonal prism. A conical cap with stalactite cornice crowns the monument. Thin, cylindrical ribs accentuating the corners of the 12 sided body, frame each of the 12 faces in the form of pointed arches. Over this row of 12 decorative, pseudo-arches, the body turns into a cylindrical form. The surfaces within the pointed arches bear rich figural and ornamental stone carvings. The figural compositions with winged lions and sphinxes, double headed eagles around a tree of life motif, may be considered as the remains of the old shamanistic symbols in the folk memory.

Anatolian Seljuk sultans preferred a rather modest life style. So, their palaces were neither colossal and imposing, nor comparable with those geometrically designed establishments of the «Old Orient» and early Islamic eras.

Seljuk palaces were composed of various *kiosks* (pavilions) placed on the most convenient points of a site without adherence to any geometrical rule.

The **Konya Palace** was situated within the inner castle. Some of its pavilions were built on the tops of the castle-towers. One of them had a single square room which opened to the east by an arch and was surrounded by a balcony on stalactite consoles. It must have been built by Sultan Kılıcaslan II in 1173-1174 and its walls were covered with glazed bricks and faience. Unfortunately, the whole citadel and palace complex of Konya have disappeared except the remains of the tower underneath this pavilion.

Recently located and then excavated two palace complexes of Sultan Alaeddin Keykubad I, **Keykubadiye**, established on the shores of an artificial lake near Kayseri in Cappadocia, and **Kubad-Abâd** on western coast of Lake Beyşehir on the Konya-Antalya road, represent the first stage of development of this certain Turkish palace type, which attains its maturity with the **Ottoman palaces of Edirne and Topkapi.**

Kubad-Abâd offers more to see and comprehend with the remains of sixteen buildings and large fortification walls surrounding the whole site. Among them the two relatively better preserved and largest ones were brought to day light by excavations. Both have central courts that were possibly covered with a dome at their tops, whereas the larger one has an extra forecourt with open top. A depot, cells, and rooms related to the kitchen surround the forecourt. The central court (or, hall) in both buildings are surrounded by various rooms. In the lake-side at east, both have an îwân which opens to the central court.

On the south of central court of the larger building is a second section with a smaller central salon and rooms surrounding it. Some art historians assume this section to be a *harem*.

The wall tiles with underglaze miniature paintings aroused a great interest among art historians as they were found most abundantly during the excavations at harem section.

In a room of harem section, fragments of stucco wall decoration were found. On one of them, a hunting scene with a mounted hunter in old Persian and early Islamic style is moulded.

The so-called **Kiz Kalesi** (Maiden's castle), a dependency of Kubad-Abâd complex, is built on a rocky islet in Lake Beyşehir. During the excavations it is understood that this was a chateau-building. In addition to various rooms and corridors, a *hamam* (bath) section with the furnace and hypocaust have been discovered. In one of its rooms, tiles with various underglaze figural paintings, such as double headed eagles have been found.

A few of the Seljuk public baths (*hamams*) remain to us, that already acquired the formal characteristics of «classic Turkish» bath of the Ottoman period. They consist of a domed-square dressing hall, tepid and hot bathing sections and a furnace room. Water is transferred to these sections through terra-cotta pipes placed in the walls, and the hot smoke from furnace is circulated underneath the paving of the hot section. Hamams are generally single buildings serving men and women at different hours or alternate days. In large centers, however, they are often double buildings repeating more or less the same plan thus offering the service simultaneously to both sexes. They are called *çifte hamam* (double bath).

Turkish architectural decoration in Asia Minor presents a unique synthesis of Asiatic Turkish and pre-Turkic Anatolian artistic traditions. Antique materials were reused in various compositions occasionally; yet, Turkish art maintained its own distinctive character; it flourished through experiment and innovation; and kept developing constantly.

The essential themes of Seljuk stone carvings are geometric interlace, angular motifs and elegant, monumental inscriptions, rosettes, stalactites in the niches or on the consols, cornices and capitals.

Although rare compared to the other themes, figural art is especially impressive in stone and stucco reliefs and palace tiles. The subjects include court nobility, astrological signs, symbolic and legendary figures such as sphinx, siren, dragon, double headed eagle and winged lions which can be regarded as the witnesses of the continuing Central Asian traditions.

The human figures in Seljuk art have full cheeks, almond shaped eyes, minute mouths and long hair. They usually are depicted sitting cross-legged, wearing caftans. Some have a halo over the head and hold symbols such as pomegranate for fertility, fish as a sign of zodiac and a music instrument. Some are sitting beside a zodiac sign.

We can claim that the famous animal-combat scenes of the Central Asian and Far Eastern cultures symbolizing the good and evil duality, reached Anatolia with the Seljuks. In the combat-scene carved on the entrance facade of **Diyarbakır Ulu Cami** for example, the bull is a representative of the enemy and darkness, whereas the lion attacking it, symbolizes power and light.

In the decoration of a few buildings, small human heads are scattered among arabesque compositions as charms and amulets. Or there are human heads in the form of rosettes, symbolizing the sun and the moon, which are mostly seen on the portals or spandrels of îwân arches. Other rosettes of purely ornamental character must represent the planets which were the symbols of the other world in old Asian mythologies.

On many tomb stones we come across a hunter on horseback holding a falcon on his wrist. These probably indicate that the deceased was a good hunter.

Lions are the most common figures in Seljuk stone carvings. They are some times shown with wings or with a dragon-head tail tip. The ones on tomb stones or mausolea, guide the soul of the dead on the journey to heaven, according to the mythology.

Double headed eagles are, at the same time, the coat of arms of the Seljuk state. It was a Central Asian tradition to regard the eagle as a protective spirit, the guardian of heaven and a symbol of light and power. In İnce Minare Museum, there is **a relief from the Konya castle** where *Assultan* (the sultan) is written between a pair of eagles.

As another typical motif, the «Tree of Life» appears in Seljuk decorations, sometime with an eagle or small birds on its branches, while in some cases a pair of lions or dragons are also added to the composition. In Central Asian mythology, the tree of life is the axis of the universe and serves as a ladder leading either to heaven or to the subterranean world.

The dragon figure is very prominent in Far Eastern and Central Asian cultures. The harmonious motion of the heavens is believed to depend on a pair of dragons of opposite sexes bound under the seven planets. Dragon figures were frequently depicted in Anatolian Seljuk art too; it is particularly dominant in fortresses such as Konya, Diyarbakır, and in caravanserais. Here, they were the talismans to ward off the enemy and illness.

Sphinxes, sirens and angels with long hair and a crown, tails and wings ending in spirals were also «protecting» the fortifications, caravanserais and palaces; but these are rare in number.

Glazed brick and tile-mosaics were used in elaborate compositions for decorating the minarets, facades looking the inner courts and inner surfaces of the buildings. This is one of the foremost features in Seljuk art. From the mid 13th century onwards, tile decoration presents a greater wealth of form, colour and design. On the contrary to the stone carvings, in tile revetments of the religious buildings, figural designs were not applied. On the other hand, the tiles with figural compositions are the most attractive features of the Seljuk palaces.

Wall tiles, found in **Konya Palace**, are the first examples of Anatolian faiences which were cut in star shape and bore miniature paintings. In these paintings, the underglaze and overglaze techniques were applied together. This is the rarest category in Asia Minor, called *Minai* tiles.

Another comparatively seldom encountered group of Anatolian Seljuk tiles is the so-called *Lustered* tile, found primarily in **Konya and Kubad-Abâd palaces**.

In the most abundantly found tiles from Seljuk palaces, polychrome figural designs were painted under a transparent glaze, on a white slip.

The themes are the same in these three groups of tiles (i.e. minai, lustered and standard type with underglaze decorations). The form of the tile itself is mostly an eight pointed star. On the majority of them, figural decorations are depicted with cold colours such as purple, green, blue and dark blue on a white ground. As the filling, or, connecting pieces, the cross shaped tiles are placed between the stars. These cross-shaped tiles are decorated with floral and geometric patterns. These none-figural designs are painted in black, under a transparent turquoise or blue glaze.

Most probably Yunus Emre had witnessed the collapse of Seljuk state in his mature years. After the death of great sultan Alaaddin Keykubad I, the Mongols marched into Asia Minor; they gained a victory over the Seljuks in 1243; the eastern half of Turkey fell to Mongols and was pillaged. Then the land disintegrated into a number of *Beyliks* (principalities). From the last quarter of the 13th century on, Turkey became a province of Mongol empire. In the central and western parts of the country, the *Beys* (princes) of various Turkoman peoples chose the path of becoming independent rulers. They engaged in battles of hegemony, sometimes with each other, sometimes against the Mongols. Furthermore, the Mamelukes who had succeeded the Ayyubids, the descendants of Great Saladin in Syro-Egyptian Sultanate, had desires on Turkey. So, a politically chaotic period had started for Turkey.

Even in this setting, the artistic and cultural activities continued creatively.

In general, the prevailing materials and craftsmanship were modest; but, the plenitude of variety and desire of experimentation did not decline, on the contrary, flourished. Until a period of maturity and a common style became predominant in Turkey, the search for innovation and variety continued in many fields, but particularly in architecture.

During the two centuries following the collapse of Seljuks, Turkoman princes and the local rich set up many structures. In these, the pre-Turkish regional features and construction techniques merged closely with the Turkish art and architecture; and they altogether directed towards the creation of a new synthesis.

In other words, the Turks became more Anatolian and Anatolia more Turkish during this period.

An interesting innovation in mosque architecture is a building type which resembles the Seljuk medreses with a domed central hall. It also has a central domed hall surrounded by îwâns and chambers. Across the entrance is the main îwân which is as large as the central hall and has a mihrab (prayer niche) since it serves as the actual prayer-hall. The other rooms around the central hall, are jurisdictional bureau, guest rooms for dervishes, classrooms, etc. So, this is a building type that houses several institutions in one block. Therefore it is called **Zawiye Mosques** (which can be translated as «convent-mosque») or «multi-functional mosque». They are very frequent in the territories of Ottoman Principality and may be considered as «condense complexes» which were the nucleus of newly built or developed cities and towns.

The largest and the second earliest of these structures is the **Hüdâvendigâr Mosque** in the Ottoman capital, Bursa. Sultan Murad I had it built in 1364. It has two storeys and in the front, a two storied *riwaq* (portico) has been created. As the Ottomans conquered the metropole region of Byzantine empire step by step, they were naturally influenced by Byzantine construction techniques and aesthetic features. In Hüdâvendigâr Mosque, the Byzantine method of wall covering and masonry can be seen very clearly: the faces have been covered by alternate rows of cut stone blocks and bricks. In addition to this, the architectural motif of a large blind arch divided into twin arches, aligned in the upper gallery of the building, became a fashion in all medieval Mediterranean structures, be it Romanesque, Byzantine or Islamic.

An old Seljuk mosque type consisting of monotonously partitioned prayer hall with equidistant piers assumed so imported a variant that it must even be considered a new type: the prayer hall became a combination of four arched baldachins crowned with a dome. The first example of this type is the **Yivli Minare Cami** in Antalya built by the Hamid Principality in 1367. The second and the most perfect example is the **Great Mosque of Bursa** which was built by Yıldırım Sultan Bayazıt I in 1396.

Without augmenting the examples of innovations, we can sum up the characteristics of this period of transition:

- All standard types of Seljuk medreses and hospitals continued to be applied during this period. New forms peculiar of this period were first seen in west Turkey.
- A new treatment of facade, the riwaqs with domed bays encircling the courts; the main îwâns becoming huge domed-cubical structures, etc., give a new architectural identity to medrese building in this period.
- Seljuk type of mausolea continued with variations in greater number whereas completely new forms were also developed.

As a final note, we can say that just as Yunus tried to understand and embrace all mankind, despite the fact that he was a local religious mystic, the Turkish people in their new home-land did not attempt to suppress the existing art and culture; on the contrary, by fusing them with their own rich traditions, they gave way to the development of an art and architecture of universal significance.

90

Contemporary Approaches to Mysticism

Prof. Dr John O'Donnell, S.J.

Introduction

My task is to share with you some thoughts on contemporary approaches to mysticism. Immediately then we must confront a problem of language and concepts: what do we mean by mysticism? Perhaps a common understanding of mysticism is that it has to do with extraordinary states of prayer which are reserved for specially graced persons. In the tradition we find reference to rare moments of special 'touches' by God. We also find the concept of visions and of a mystical marriage in which the mystic knows himself or herself to be in union with the divine in a way which transcends all human powers of description. A common feature of this approach to mysticism is that all sensible images are left behind. The world has no value in comparison with the experience of the divine. In some cases of Christian mysticism it seems that even Jesus himself is left behind and the soul is given an immediate union with the abyss of the Godhead. For the German mystic, Meister Eckhart (c.1260-1327), for example, even the Trinity of persons exists only on the surface of the Absolute. Although each human being should find his personality in Christ, Eckhart embraces an extreme form of apophatism according to which God is ultimately No-thing and one is called to renounce all in order to enter into the depths of the 'silent Godhead'.

The approach which I would like to develop here is different. I would like to go back to the root of the word mysticism, namely mystery. According to Karl Rahner, God is the one and only Mystery of Christian faith. All the

91

doctrines of faith are ultimately ordered to this one Mystery.[1] In this sense Rahner speaks of all Christian language about God as mystagogic. Our language about God, our prayer and liturgy, should lead us to the Mystery. For Rahner, Christianity is basically about the revelation of the Mystery. Christian faith proclaims that God, the Holy Mystery, has wanted to reveal himself and draw near to us in Jesus Christ. Rahner's approach is similar to that of St. Paul who often speaks about the Mystery. In the Letter to the Ephesians, for example, Paul says that in Christ God has made known the mystery of his will (Eph. 1:19). This mystery consists in the divine plan for the fullness of time, namely to unite all persons and things in Christ. Later in chapter 3 Paul speaks in a similar way when he prays that his Christians might be strengthened through the Spirit in the inner man and that Christ may dwell in their hearts so that they might comprehend what is the breadth and length, the height and depth, that is, that they might know the love of God which surpasses understanding and so be filled with the fullness of God.

Two things strike us here immediately. Mysticism is not some privileged access to God. It is not some special esoteric realm of divine knowledge. Rather it is knowledge of God which is unveiled in Christ for all to see and contemplate. Secondly, Paul seems to presuppose that this is not an experience for the few, rather it is open to all Christians. Every man and woman is called to union with Christ and hence to a knowledge of God, indeed to be filled with the fullness of God.

The Experience of Jesus

When we look to the experience of Jesus, the first thing we note is the tremendous claim he makes about himself. We are immediately struck by the fact that he claims to be the bearer of a unique revelation. In Matt. 11:27 Jesus says,

> All things have been delivered to me by my Father; and no one knows the Son except the Father and no one knows the Father except the Son and anyone to whom the Son chooses to reveal him.

What does Jesus mean here by 'all things'? We can probably make a link with his Kingdom-preaching. Jesus has received the mission from the Father to make present his rule on earth. Mark 1:15 sums up Jesus's preaching in this way:

---

[1] See Karl Rahner, "The Concept of Mystery in Catholic Theology," *Theological Investigations* 4 (London: Darton, Longman and Todd, 1966), pp. 36-73.

The Kingdom of God is at hand; repent, and believe the gospel. Jesus in his life and ministry makes present God's reign.

The fourth gospel, in the light of Jesus's death and resurrection, interprets Jesus's relation to the Father not only in earthly but also in heavenly terms. In the famous last supper discourse of John 17, Jesus prays that the disciples be initiated into the very union with the Father which he enjoys as Son. The goal of his mission is summed up in the words:

Thou, Father in me and I in them. (Jn. 17:23)

Another aspect of Jesus's life which strikes us is his obedience. Jesus interprets his union with the Father in terms of his mission. According to the fourth gospel Jesus is the eternal Son of the Father made flesh. As such Jesus knows his divine origin. He lives out of this origin. This origin is the source of everything he says and does. The Swiss theologian, Hans Urs von Balthasar, says that Jesus does not live from his origin as from a past event, a distant memory. Rather he is continually present to his origin. According to Balthasar, if we ask about the 'where' of Jesus, we must respond that his 'where' is always in the Father. But this is true whether for his pre-existent state of divine Sonship or for his life on earth.[2] At any moment he can find the Father, for he is prompt to listen to the Father and to do his will. This is a constant theme of the gospels. As a boy in the temple, Jesus must occupy himself with his Father's business (Lk. 2:41-52). In the garden of Gethsemane, faced with the bitter cup of suffering and death, Jesus prays, "Not my will but thine be done." (Mk. 14:36). The fourth gospel sums it up when Jesus declares,

I have food to eat of which you do not know. My food is to do the will of him who sent me, and to accomplish his work. (Jn. 4:32-34

A final point which is most important for our purposes: Jesus's relationship to the world. There is not the least hint in the gospels that Jesus has to flee the world to find God. In the midst of his busy ministry and even in the darkness of his suffering he finds God because he loves the Father and is constantly ready to do his will. Hence being in the world creates no problems for finding the presence of God. With the doctrine of the Incarnation, Christians believe that Jesus has sanctified every dimension of human life. God has entered into our world of space and time, into our history, and redeemed them from within. We Christians look on this man Jesus and see the glory of God. But since Jesus is

---

[2] See Hans Urs von Balthasar, *The Christian State of Life* (San Francisco: St. Ignatius Press, 1983), pp. 183ff.

really a man and since he has revealed God to us in the course of a human pilgrimage, he gives us an example of how we should live our human journey. Being in him we have the firm hope that it is possible to find God's presence in the midst of our daily routine.

Christian Mysticism: The Search for an Equilibrium

In the light of the experience of Jesus, two things at least seem decisive: first, the fact that he lived fully immersed in the world, second, his clear teaching that the core of discipleship consists in love:

> A new commandment I give to you, that you love one another.
> (Jn. 13:34)

In the immediate centuries following Christ, however, we see a major development. Christian faith underwent an encounter with the mystical tradition of the Orient and especially with Hellenistic philosophy. Philosophically the most important figure is Plotinus (c.205-270). What we see here is the notion of ascent. The soul must purify itself of all attachment to creatures, of all its passions in order to make its ascent to the One. For Plotinus the One is absolutely beyond all plurality. The soul, as it makes its way to the One, loses itself in God, leaving the world behind. The asceticism of Neo-Platonism is basically anti-worldly. The greatest weakness of this system from a philosophical point of view is that it fails to explain how the world came to be at all. How explain the descending movement from the One to the Many?

I would say that Christian monasticism inherited a number of negative features from this type of spirituality. In this context I would like to reflect briefly upon one of the most important figures of Eastern monasticism, Evagrius of Pontus who lived in the fourth century (346-399). Evagrius is one of the key figures of Christian spirituality, for his writings had a profound influence not only upon the East but also upon the West. His doctrine contains two parts. One is more practical and offers marvellous intuitions about the nature of the discernment of spirits. The other part is more speculative and is more questionable as regards offering a balanced doctrine of Christian spirituality. There is no doubt that Evagrius is a mystic, but can we say that he is a Christian mystic? One notable spiritual writer, Hans Urs von Balthasar, has serious doubts about this.[3]

---

[3] See Hans Urs von Balthasar, "Metaphysik und Mystik des Evagrius Ponticus," in *Zeitschrift für Aszese und Mystik* (Innsbruck, 1939), p. 40.

The difficulty is typically Neo-Platonic. For Evagrius the goal of the spiritual life in gnosis, knowledge of the Absolute. This can only be reached by spirit. Hence the passions and everything bodily must be renounced as impeding gnosis. The ascent takes place by turning away from all creatures. No image, no form, no phantasm can lead us to the Abyss of God. The goal must be achieved by emptiness. All multiplicity must give way to the One. Evagrius recognized that the Logos or the divine Word is the archetype containing all the divine ideas. All worldly realities reflect the divine archetype. But since the Word contains within itself multiplicity, the soul must move beyond the Kingdom of the Son to that of the Father, in other words to the Kingdom of indivisible unity.

Another key difficulty for Evagrius's thought is the role of love. Obviously, Evagrius recognizes the need for love of neighbour. But the neighbour is not loved for himself or herself. Rather the neighbour is the occasion for the purifying of the passions. Mystics such as Evagrius often speak of ecstasy, of standing outside of oneself. But Balthasar questions whether their spirituality offers a true ecstasy or is it rather an entasy – a turning within.[4] In summary, he questions whether in Evagrius there is a genuine recognition of the Thou, or is God merely another word for the depths of the I?

We see similar tensions reflected in the great Spanish mystic of the sixteenth century, John of the Cross (1542-1591). However, John has been declared a doctor of the church, hence the church officially recognizes that his doctrine offers a balanced path of Christian ascent to God. Let us then look for a moment at how he deals with the question of the ascent.[5]

There is a radicality about John's thought which is similar to that of Evagrius. He too insists on a strict *via negativa*. God is beyond all images and concepts. So one must leap into the dark night of unknowing. But there is also an important difference. The centre of John's thought is the crucified Christ. He has been grasped by Christ's love in such a profound manner that he is enabled to make the leap of faith. Faith for John lies between two illuminations. There is the first illumination of love when one is grasped by Christ's self-gift. On the basis of this illumination the Christian embarks on the way of negation hoping for a new illumination after the process of purification has been completed. The

---

[4] See Hans Urs von Balthasar, *The Glory of the Lord, A Theological Aesthetics, Vol. 1: Seeing the Form* (Edinburgh; T. and T. Clark, 1982), p. 267.

[5] In my presentation of John of the Cross, I am following Hans Urs von Balthasar, *The Glory of the Lord III: Studies in Theological Styles: Lay Styles* (Edinburgh: T. and T. Clark, 1986), pp. 105-171.

Christological centre of John's spirituality is beyond dispute. In one of the most magnificent chapters of the *Ascent to Mount Carmel* he hears God say to him,

> I have already told you everything in my Word, who is my Son. I have nothing more to reveal, no further answer to give you, there is nothing to add to him. Fasten your eyes on him alone, because in him I have spoken and revealed everything. *Ipsum audite* (listen to him).[6]

John's approach to the *via negativa* is paradoxical. Faith is darkness and yet John identifies faith and contemplation. But in the theological tradition contemplation is *theoria* or vision. Do we not have here a contradiction? No, for by faith John understands the surrender of love. Insofar as faith is love, love sees the object of its choice, for the believer has first been grasped by God. Insofar as faith is the act of a creature, it is shrouded in darkness. What is darkness for the believer is light for God. Paradoxically, then, the way of faith is "vision in the mode of non-vision."

Another important dimension of John's spirituality is the place of the creation in his vision. As part of the *via negativa* creatures must be left behind. However, we must not forget that John's mysticism is not philosophical. It is theological. Its starting point is being grasped by God's love. Hence in the end what John advocates is a new understanding of the creation. One should not love the creation for its own sake but one can rediscover the values and beauty of the created world within the perspective of the vision of God's love. As he says in *The Living Flame of Love*,

> Although the soul in this state (of contemplation) is indeed aware that all things are distinct from God insofar as they have created being, and sees them in him by their power, their root and their tension, nonetheless, she knows precisely that God, by his being all these things with infinite eminence, is such that she knows these things better in God's being than in themselves.[7]

Paradoxically, then, the creature is not left behind on the ascent but is rediscovered in God. This fact serves to explain the basic dialectic of John's theological existence, that he expresses the radicality of the *via negativa* in the incandescence of lyric poetry.

Still, as Balthasar points out, something is left unsaid in John. Where is the role of the neighbour in the ascent to God? Where is the apostolic dimension, the call to service? For all the subtlety of John's approach, there does seem

---

[6] See *Ascent to Mount Carmel* II, 22 as cited by Balthasar, *ibid.*, pp. 162-163.
[7] *The Living Flame of Love*, IV, 5 as cited by Balthasar, *ibid.*, p. 149.

to be an important element missing. Let us turn, then, to Ignatius of Loyola (1491-1556) to see how he offers us a mysticism of mission.

St. Ignatius is especially noteworthy for offering a clear response to the tension we have seen in the Christian tradition between flight from the world and love of creation. In an article on the Ignatian mysticism of joy in the world, Karl Rahner has shown how Ignatius stands clearly in the monastic tradition.[8] The only way to God is flight from the world in the sense that God is beyond all creatures. God is the transcendent Mystery *par excellence*, wholly other, radically different from the created world. But precisely this transcendent otherness of God allows him to enter into the world, to become incarnate and even to identify with our suffering on the cross. The Christian, then, who follows Jesus, places his faith and hope in the God beyond the world but at the same time like Jesus he seeks to find God's presence in the midst of daily life.

According to Christian faith, God enters the world because he is moved by the plight of sinful human beings. The Christian who follows Jesus is likewise moved by the situation of his suffering brothers and sisters, by their needs on the temporal and spiritual level. So he or she awaits in receptivity to be sent by the Father.

St. Ignatius offered the church the nucleus of his spiritual vision in his little book, *The Spiritual Exercises*. Basically the goal of the Exercises is to help a Christian achieve spiritual freedom. On the one hand, the retreatant making the Exercises seeks to be free to accept any mission which God wishes to propose to him. This mission will place the totality of his life at the disposition of his brothers and sisters. A phrase which recurs repeatedly in Ignatius's writings is "to help souls." The spirituality of the Exercises is radically apostolic.

On the other hand, once the mission has been accepted, the Exercises lead the Christian to ever greater freedom, that is, to an ever greater ability to find God in the daily routine. Since the created order is good and since God deigned to become incarnate in it, there is no reason in principle why God should not be found there. The only reason why we fail to see God objectively present in our world is our egoism. We are so filled with ourselves that our vision of God is blocked.

Hence for Ignatius the key to mysticism is purification of selfishness. He recommends a type of prayer in which each day we examine our lives to see

---

[8] See Karl Rahner, "The Ignatian Mysticism of Joy in the World," *Theological Investigations* 3 (London: Darton, Longman and Todd, 1967), pp. 277-293.

where we find God and where we fail to find him. The Christian asks himself: where has God been and where have I been? In this way he grows in what we could call the mysticism of decision-making. As he is purified of his selfishness, the world becomes ever more charged with the glory of God. The more the Christian grows in this purification, the more he lives what Ignatius calls consolation, that is,

> an interior movement in the soul, by which it is inflamed with love of its Creator and Lord, and as a consequence, can love no creature on the face of the earth for its own sake, but only in the Creator of them all. (no. 316).

In short, he learns to find God in all things.

Contemporary Trends in Mysticism

Although our reflections thus far have been largely historical, they have been guided by the central question which remains highly actual today: what is mysticism? The English theologian, Nicholas Lash, in his stimulating book *Easter in Ordinary* speaks of two kinds of mysticism; exclusive and inclusive. Exclusive mysticism refers to intense private experiences of God which a person has in his or her solitude. Inclusive mysticism refuses to speak of an experience of God apart from a concrete community which lives out of a specific historical tradition. Exclusive mysticism is oriented toward extraordinary religious experiences. Inclusive mysticism has as its goal: to find God in the ordinary.

In Lash's book he spends hundred pages discussing the philosopher William James's understanding of religious experience. James in his classic, *Varieties of Religious Experience*, is not interested in the common folk, those who belong to an institutional church and live from a tradition. He is interested in the pattern-setters, in the religious genius. In James's opinion the great religious geniuses were loners. He writes,

> The religious experience which we are studying is that which lives itself out within the private breast. First-hand individual experience of this kind has always appeared as a heretical sort of innovation to those who witnessed its birth. Naked comes it into the world and lonely; and it has always, for a time at least, driven him who had it into the wilderness, often into the literal wilderness out of doors, where the Buddha, Jesus, Mohammed, St. Francis, George Fox, and so many others had to go.[9]

---

[9] William James, *Varieties of Religious Experience* as cited by Lash, *Easter in Ordinary* (London, SCM Press, 1988), p. 55.

For James these pace setters have experiences of which the rest of us are not capable. Hence religious experience is reserved for the few. The others can only rely on their testimony.

What does all this have to do with mysticism? James identifies religious experience with mysticism and for him mysticism is practically another word for the paranormal. For James there is some dimension of reality which eludes most of us but a few have found it and can tell us about it. Lash argues that in fact many of our contemporaries work with this understanding of religious experience. They see religion as having to do with the exotic. And since many persons would say they have never had such an exotic experience, they can easily be led to believe that they are irreligious.

But there is another approach to mysticism, the one which I have tried to outline in this paper, that experience lived by Jesus and witnessed to by such a great saint and mystic as Ignatius of Loyola. It begins with the fact that God is to be found where he makes himself known. The experience of God is firmly embedded in an historical tradition. Jesus, to be sure, had a unique experience of God but this experience would never have been possible without the centuries-long mediation of the experience of God in Israel's history. Moreover, the mystical experience of God is not something solitary. It is not closed off from the community. Rather the experience of God can be mediated through community and through institutions. Hence it is not just for the few. Any member of the community can make the experience of God his own and interiorize it even to horizons without limit. Finally, the experience of God embedded in a religious tradition does not lead a man or a woman away from the world. Rather, it helps them to see the world in a new light. As one theologian has put it, prayer does not draw us away from the routine but rather leads to "illumination of the commonplace."[10]

In summary, then, much reflection today about the Christian understanding of mysticism leads us back to the central questions: what is mysticism? what is a specifically Christian mysticism? In my opinion there seems to be a consensus that mysticism, at least for a Christian, is not to be found in extraordinary experiences of God that lead one to a solitary adventure of flight to the Absolute. Rather Christian mysticism is the exploration of what can happen to a Christian when he lives out his particular religious tradition and his particular faith commitments to its depths.

---

[10] Noel-Dermot O'Donoghue, *Heaven in Ordinary* (Springfield, Ill. 1979), p. 192 as cited by Lash, *op. cit.*, p. 294.

Pubblicazioni periodiche dell'Editrice
Pontificia Università Gregoriana

ARCHIVUM
HISTORIAE PONTIFICIAE

rivista annuale di Storia Ecclesiastica

abbonamento vol. 32/1994: L. 110.000 – US $ 100.00

GREGORIANUM

rivista trimestrale di Teologia e Filosofia

abbonamento 1995: L. 80.000 – US $ 75.00

PERIODICA
DE RE CANONICA

rivista trimestrale di Diritto Canonico

abbonamento 1995: L. 80.000 – US $ 75.00

Amministrazione: Piazza della Pilotta 35 – 00187 Roma
Tel. 06/678.15.67 – Fax 06/678.05.88 – ccp 34903005

Riproduzione anastatica: 22 luglio 1994
Tipografia Poliglotta della Pontificia Università Gregoriana
Piazza della Pilotta, 4 – 00187 Roma

PONTIFICIA UNIVERSITÀ GREGORIANA

EDIZIONI 1994

NOVITÀ

ANALECTA GREGORIANA

265. DE LIMA João Tavares: «*Tu serás chamado Κηφᾶς*». *Estudo exegético sobre Pedro no quarto evangelho.*
pp. XXIV-392.   ISBN 88-7652-667-6.   Lit. 54.000

266. PAVANELLO Pierantonio: *Il requisito della perpetuità nell'incapacità di assumere le obbligazioni essenziali del matrimonio.*
ISBN 88-7652-672-2. in corso di stampa

INCULTURATION

XV. DINH DUC DAO Joseph: *Preghiera rinnovata per una nuova era missionaria in Asia.*
pp. XII-216.   ISBN 88-7652-673-0.   Lit. 24.000

XVI. AA. VV.: *Yunus Emre: Spiritual Experience and Culture.*
pp. VI-102.   ISBN 88-7652-674-9.   Lit. 13.000

STUDIA MISSIONALIA

43. AA. VV.: *Interfaith Dialogue.*
pp. X-366.   ISBN 88-7652-669-2.   Lit. 65.000

FUORI COLLANA

GHIRLANDA Gianfranco (a cura di): *Punti fondamentali sulla vita consacrata.*
pp. X-178.   ISBN 88-7652-670-6.   Lit. 20.000

HENNESSY Anne: *The Galilee of Jesus.*
pp. X-78.   ISBN 88-7652-666-8.   Lit. 15.000

LÓPEZ-GAY Jesús (a cura di): *La missione della Chiesa nel mondo di oggi.*
pp. 76.   ISBN 88-7652-671-4.   Lit. 8.500

COEDIZIONI

TEANI Maurizio: *Corporeità e Risurrezione. L'interpretazione di 1 Corinti 15,35-49 nel Novecento.*
pp. 336.   ISBN 88-7652-668-4.   Lit. 50.000

AA. VV.

RELIGIOUS SECTS
AND MOVEMENTS

(STUDIA MISSIONALIA, n. 41)

1992. pp. VIII-392   L. 65.000

ISBN 88-7652-650-1

EDITRICE PONTIFICIA UNIVERSITÀ GREGORIANA – ROMA

AA. VV.

THEOLOGY OF
RELIGIONS

(STUDIA MISSIONALIA, n. 42)

1993. pp. VIII-396   L. 65.000

ISBN 88-7652-657-9

EDITRICE PONTIFICIA UNIVERSITÀ GREGORIANA

Amministrazione: Piazza della Pilotta 35 – 00187 Roma – Italia
Tel. 06/678.15.67 – Fax 06/678.05.88 – ccp 34903005